SENATOR
PRESSLER

An Independent Mission to Save Our Democracy

SENATOR LARRY PRESSLER

I0161711

PUBLISHED BY

F⊕RTIS

A NONFICTION IMPRINT FROM ADDUCENT
WWW.ADDUCENT.CO

TITLES DISTRIBUTED IN
NORTH AMERICA
UNITED KINGDOM
WESTERN EUROPE
SOUTH AMERICA
AUSTRALIA

TO CONTACT SENATOR PRESSLER ABOUT SPEAKING ENGAGEMENTS

CONTACT INFORMATION:

SENATOR LARRY PRESSLER (RET.)
THE PLAZA, SUITE 504
800 25TH STREET, NW
WASHINGTON, DC 20037-2208
LPRESSLER@LARRYPRESSLER.COM
WWW.LARRYPRESSLER.COM

SENATOR PRESSLER

An Independent
Mission to Save
Our Democracy

SENATOR LARRY PRESSLER

SENATOR LARRY PRESSLER
An Independent Mission to Save Our Democracy
Larry Pressler

Copyright © 2016. All rights reserved. No part of this book may be reproduced or transmitted in any form or by any means, electronic or mechanical. Including photocopying, recording or by any information storage and retrieval system, without written permission from the author, except for brief quotations as would be used in a review.

ISBN 9781937592585
Library of Congress Catalog Number: 2016931953

Published by Fortis (a nonfiction imprint from Adducent)
Jacksonville, Florida
www.Adducent.co

Published in the United States of America

All statements of fact, opinion, or analysis expressed are those of the author and do not reflect the official positions or views of the publisher. Nothing in the contents should be construed as asserting or implying authentication of information or endorsement of the author's views. This book and subjects discussed within are designed to provide the author's opinion about the subject matter covered and is for informational purposes only.

DEDICATION

I dedicate this book to my beloved wife, Harriet. She is probably the only woman in the world who could put up with me all these years! We have had many wonderful experiences and fun together. In the past two years, she has tolerated this old man attempting a comeback to the U.S. Senate and becoming a member of the Mormon Church.

When I told her I wished to run for the U.S. Senate again, she suggested I see a psychiatrist. So I went to see my friend, Dr. Ron Smith. He said, "Larry, you have real chutzpah! At age seventy-two, you have the courage to run for the U.S. Senate as an Independent!" To my surprise, he was delighted with my candidacy and became my first contributor. He immediately wrote me a $2,600 campaign contribution (the largest amount he could legally give).

So Harriet's advice was another of her deft moves in our relationship. And during this campaign, and in earlier campaigns, she was right there helping as much as she could.

She has been my best friend, my spiritual and soulmate, and my fellow soldier in our efforts to serve God.

I would also extend this dedication to our daughter Laura, her husband, Robert, and our four grandchildren, Ryan, Julia, Addison, and Bethany. They give me hope for the future.

TABLE OF CONTENTS

PREFACE

In 2014, I ran for the United States Senate in South Dakota as an Independent. I had previously served three full terms in the U.S. Senate (1979–1997) and two terms in the U.S. House of Representatives (1975–1979) as a Republican. Why did I run as an Independent? People would ask me, "Why do you want to go back to the poisonous atmosphere in the U.S. Senate?"

I was upset with the direction that our country was heading—politically and morally. We seemed to have lost our spiritual, fiscal, and ethical core. I wanted to do something about it. I felt driven, spiritually and in a civic sense, to raise my voice once more.

My friend Tom Brokaw, a classmate of mine whom I met at the University of South Dakota in the early 1960s, wrote a famous book called *The Greatest Generation*. It is the story of the dedicated people who won World War II and rebuilt America after the war. I feel strongly that my generation has squandered this great inheritance—in fact, I almost named this book *The Squandering Generation*. I wanted to go back to the Senate to try to change the direction of our country.

My generation's big problem *was* and *is* Vietnam. It tore us apart emotionally. Those who did not serve or evaded the draft feel guilty about it, as they know someone poorer—and probably a minority—served in their place. Those of us who did serve have always been trapped with the categorization that we supported the war—when in fact, we just felt we were doing our duty to our

1

country. The general public feels deeply conflicted and is trying to make up for it. Why? Partly because the demonstrations against the Vietnam War were not against the war itself—they were mostly against the draft system. When the all-volunteer service was adopted, all the antiwar movement evaporated. Later the Iraq wars presented at least as many reasons to protest as the Vietnam War—but there was no draft. Hence, no antiwar protests.

Our generation has yet to come to honesty about the Vietnam War. To help heal those wounds, we must have major innovations in our political system. I knew I couldn't make a difference serving as a traditional Republican or Democrat within the two-party system, so I designed and embarked on my own independent, innovative crusade.

Many thought that this was an audacious idea. But this was something that was stirring in my blood—I was called to do it. With a dedicated team, I set out to design what we called "an innovative, ideal campaign." It was my dream to be free to say anything I believed in a campaign: free to state my convictions, free to follow my inner spiritual drive, and free at last not to be forced to stay within a political party's talking points. I always had an independent streak, and it had cost me advancement in my Republican Party in the past. In 2014, I wanted to be *free at last* to be a *real* Independent!

So I embarked on this journey, not knowing where it would take me. The boldness and difficulty involved in running for the U.S. Senate again at the age of seventy-two took all the spiritual and mental strength I could muster. I prayed on it a lot. And reading my favorite poem, *Invictus,* always renewed my spirit:

Invictus

Out of the night that covers me,
Black as the Pit from pole to pole,

I thank whatever gods may be
For my unconquerable soul.

In the fell clutch of circumstance
I have not winced nor cried aloud.
Under the bludgeonings of chance
My head is bloody, but unbowed.

Beyond this place of wrath and tears
Looms but the Horror of the shade,
And yet the menace of the years
Finds, and shall find, me unafraid.

It matters not how strait the gate,
How charged with punishments the scroll.
I am the master of my fate,
I am the captain of my soul.

--William Ernest Henley

Along the way, we *did* change politics in my state and we *did* make history. This book tells of my personal story and this remarkable journey.

PROLOGUE

American Hustle–ABSCAM
Bribery Scandal Revisited

Curiously, a movie release helped me make my decision to run for the U.S. Senate again after less than two decades out of office. In 2013, *American Hustle* hit the movie theaters—with a big Hollywood promotional campaign and multiple Academy Award nominations. I played a real-life role in the subject of this movie, "ABSCAM." Suddenly, my phone was ringing off the hook—national media wanted my comment on an event that had given me my national fame in 1979. To understand the historic significance of this event, we need to go back more than three decades.

In 1979, I was briefly a candidate for president of the United States. My platform was based principally on how we could improve treatment of our beleaguered Vietnam veterans. I was having a hard time getting any traction with this issue, although my campaign generated much enthusiasm among my fellow Vietnam veterans. Running a national campaign for the presidency of the United States was exhausting—I gave speeches in more than thirty states. And I had to raise money—lots of money— from people I didn't know. It was very different from politics in my home state of South Dakota, where I knew everyone. Therefore, with few deep-pocketed supporters, when one of my volunteers informed me that three political action committees

(PACs) were eager to meet me and talk about contributing to my campaign, I agreed to visit them at their various locations. In retrospect, it was probably too good to be true.

I recall so vividly the events of that day. For one of the PACs, we drove to a two-story red brick colonial home on fashionable W Street. Inside, the house was furnished with exquisite antiques, elegant chandeliers, and, as I would later learn, a battery of hidden television cameras and microphones. Unwittingly, my inexperienced volunteer had led me into a hornets' nest—the most elaborate undercover sting operation ever launched by the FBI.

It was code-named "ABSCAM"—short for "Arab scam"— and it involved months of hard work by more than one hundred FBI agents in an extensive series of hoaxes and disguises. One of the FBI imposters I met that day was a swarthy man who appeared to be from the Middle East. He told me that he represented a prominent sheik who was seeking entry to the United States for himself and a number of his associates. The sheik needed special bills passed by Congress in order to avoid the usual immigration procedures.

Growing suspicious, I asked the "sheik's" representative about his political action committee, or PAC.

"What's a PAC?" he said with a straight face.

He had never heard of a PAC, but offered to give me $50,000 if I would play ball.

"We want to invest in your [state], but we don't want to do it under our name," he said. "We want to do it in somebody else's name."

At that moment, I responded very clearly (as I later saw my words verbatim on video tape): "Wait a minute!" I said. "What you are suggesting may be illegal. It would not be proper for me to do anything in return for a campaign contribution, so I would not make any promises."

It wasn't until a couple of months later, when the ABSCAM story burst onto the front pages of American newspapers, that I learned the full scope of the FBI sting.

Seven members of the House of Representatives, two dozen state and local officials and their corrupt cronies, and another U.S. senator had visited the "sheik's" representative and agreed to perform special favors in return for bribes. Many were ultimately indicted and sent to jail. It turned out that I was the only public official who had flatly refused to take the bait.

The 1987 *Congressional Quarterly*'s book, *Politics in America—The 100th Congress*, described the incident this way: "But the presidential campaign did give Pressler a round of priceless national attention. Late in 1979, FBI agents posing as Arab sheiks invited him to a Georgetown house to offer him a bribe, knowing that he badly needed money for his presidential effort. It was part of the ABSCAM corruption probe. Pressler refused to have anything to do with the offer, and stormed out of the meeting. It briefly made him a minor hero. 'I turned down an illegal contribution,' he said afterward. 'Where have we come to if that's considered heroic?'"

The secretly recorded ABSCAM videotapes were played on national television, and for a time I was hailed as a hero. Syndicated cartoonist Jim Berry drew a caricature of me being greeted by the Greek philosopher Diogenes, who famously carried a lantern throughout the ancient world searching for an honest man. "SENATOR PRESSLER?" read the caption under Berry's cartoon. "I AM DIOGENES. I'VE BEEN LOOKING FOR YOU."

Walter Cronkite singled me out for praise on the *CBS Evening News*. *The Washington Post* ran a front-page story about the "special moment in which Sen. Larry Pressler (R-SD) tells the undercover agent, in effect, to take their sting and stick it."

The tributes continued to pile up. My former professor, Alan Dershowitz, used me as an exemplar of civic virtue in his

Harvard Law School class. Many law students have asked me, "How did you say just the right thing? Where did that come from? You must have learned that at Harvard Law School or when you were a Rhodes Scholar at Oxford." "No," I always reply. "My values came from my hardscrabble life on a midwestern farm and the moral and spiritual guidance of my parents."

Judge George C. Pratt, who reviewed the ABSCAM cases when they came up for appeal, declared: "Pressler, particularly, acted as citizens have a right to expect their elected representatives to act. He showed a clear awareness of the line between proper and improper conduct, and despite his confessed need for campaign money, and despite the additional attractiveness to him of the payment offered, he nevertheless refused to cross into impropriety."

Berry's World

This cartoon ran nationwide in most of the leading papers in the United States and abroad. It is still reprinted occasionally and gave me the nickname "Diogenes" for a time. Illustration courtesy of Jim Berry.

© 1980 by NEA, Inc.

"SENATOR PRESSLER? I AM DIOGENES. I'VE BEEN LOOKING FOR YOU."

FOR SENATOR LARRY PRESSLER: WITH MY VERY BEST WISHES — Jim Berry

Later, when the bipartisan Senate Select Committee on Ethics reviewed my involvement in ABSCAM, it sent me a letter stating that my rejection of the ABSCAM scheme was "immediate, forthright and unequivocal... In this test of integrity, your action upheld the honor of the United States Senate."

In spite of all the accolades, I didn't feel like a hero. On the contrary, I was deeply embarrassed by the attention I received. After all, where I come from, South Dakota, your neighbors expect you to do the right thing, and they don't pat you on the back just for being a decent guy.

Judge Pratt's ruling is still the prevalent law on all types of entrapment cases. Entrapment policy always cites the "Pressler standard" that almost every law student in the world reads. It is very simple—you *can* turn down a bribe. Sometimes in life, one event can define you—and that event was a defining moment of my career.

In the wake of ABSCAM, I couldn't help but wonder: What has America come to when turning down an illegal bribe is considered a heroic act? In the three decades since ABSCAM, that question has continued to gnaw at me as I've watched things go from bad to worse in our country.

I was—and still am—angry, disgusted, heartbroken, and just downright mad about the dysfunction of the two parties in Washington, D.C. The Republicans and Democrats in Washington are more loyal to their political party than they are to their voters. I wanted to figure out how to break the stranglehold of the insane partisan fighting that is dragging our nation down.

So as I approached my seventy-first birthday and reflected on a life of public service—two tours of duty in Vietnam, three years in the State Department, four years in the House of Representatives, and eighteen years in the Senate—I decided to try once more to do something about it.

CHAPTER 1

An Audacious Idea—
The Independent U.S. Senate Run

A udacious! Unrealistic! Unprecedented! Idealistic! Challenging! Unbridled chutzpah! That's what almost everyone said about my Independent campaign bid for the U.S. Senate in 2014. Although I was in good health, I was seventy-two years old. Although I had served in the Senate for three terms and was an experienced legislator, I had not been in public office since 1997. Although I was always a South Dakota resident, very active in the state, and was well known to its voters, many South Dakotans under the age of thirty-six did not know me because I had been out of office for almost two decades.

Like many Americans, I had become profoundly troubled by the disease that has paralyzed Washington. I continue to be troubled by the decline in our moral standards nationally, by the weakening of our work ethic, the erosion of public integrity, and the waning of the worth of public service. My concern encompasses not only corrupt practices in government circles, but also the decline in civic participation, and the corruptive role unlimited campaign spending plays in elections. And then there is the deplorable behavior among people who run our major institutions—journalists, businessmen, labor leaders, college presidents, research scientists, charity trustees—to say nothing of elected members of Congress and administration officials.

That is not to say there aren't many honorable and dedicated public servants whom I admire. There are many political figures I wanted to go back to the Senate to emulate, including personal friends such as Ronald Reagan, Howard Baker, Harry Reid, Angus King, and George McGovern.

Ever since I left the U.S. Senate in 1997, people would come up to me at airports to tell me that they wished I were still their senator. I realized that a lot of this was simple politeness. In early 2013, an unusual number of events coincided to persuade me to run for the Senate one more time.

In March of 2013, Democratic Senator Tim Johnson who, ironically, narrowly defeated me in my senatorial bid for reelection for a fourth term in 1996, announced he would not seek reelection in 2014. This created an open Senate seat in our state—the first time since 1978.

In light of this rare opportunity, many friends from across the state increasingly and more ardently asked me if I would consider running again. Farmers and the many business people with whom I serve on the Farmers Union board, students and professors at the various South Dakota colleges where I teach, and political leaders on both sides of the aisle were all encouraging me.

They wanted me to run for practical reasons. I had done an enormous amount of legislation and work on special projects for South Dakota's economy, infrastructure, and the Native American community. Citizens wanted that level of constituent services restored. Also, I could take my seniority back to the U.S. Senate and immediately become one of the most senior senators. South Dakotans wanted a powerful senator—and they asked me to run again.

During my previous years in the Senate, I had worked on a number of important projects for my state. Just to name a few, they included: better air service to South Dakota; increased rail capabilities to export our state's agricultural products; water pipelines; enhancement of small businesses; the expansion of Ellsworth Air Force Base; the establishment of the Center for Earth Resources Observation (EROS)—a worldwide federal mapping agency; improved conditions for the Native Americans—including efforts against fetal alcohol syndrome; and the creation of certain scientific grants reserved to smaller universities.

I had also worked on many national and international issues as a member of the Senate Foreign Relations Committee, including the "Pressler Amendment" which fundamentally redefined our whole nuclear weapons and arms control program. I served as chairman of the Senate Commerce Committee and authored the Telecommunications Act of 1996, legislation that laid the groundwork for the Internet.

During my eighteen years out of public office, I was a professor and a columnist/contributor to South Dakota's newspapers. In early 2013, I wrote a series of articles expressing my criticism of our nation's exorbitant overseas military spending. As a Vietnam combat veteran, my column expressed support for military reforms that would make us just as effective overseas at a much lower cost. I also expressed opposition to the foreign invasions, such as Iraq, that our military-industrial state seems to promote. I was surprised at the number of people who called me to voice their support for my position and to ask me to run for public office again.

One issue that inspired me was a proposal to establish a series of treatment centers around the country to help veterans suffering from post-traumatic stress disorder (PTSD). I suffer from PTSD myself and I wanted to weigh in on this idea. I had sponsored some of the original legislation to get PTSD listed as a disability and worked extensively with veterans in a volunteer capacity. If elected to the Senate, I wanted to introduce a bill that would make it easier for veterans to get support for their treatment and not hurt their careers.

I supported a proposal to build one of these centers at the existing veterans' hospital in Hot Springs, South Dakota. This small town is about an hour and a half from the Rapid City airport. It is a serene setting in the mountains in the southern Black Hills with a river and a small golf course.

Accordingly, I began to tell people that I would be willing to serve again, but not as a traditional Republican or Democrat. I only wanted to go back to Washington as an Independent, where I would not have to submit to the power of special interests in one of the Senate party caucuses. To be honest, in my soul, I was seeking a role where I could still be useful in public service—but I did not want to be handcuffed by our deadlocked political system. *And that meant becoming an Independent U.S. senator.* I began to believe that this was the time and the opportunity to do it.

I was honored for my service as a Vietnam veteran in 2014 by Donald A. Dahlin, the South Dakota Veterans of Foreign Wars state commander. Photo - Larry Pressler

A key part of my belief, and desire to run again, was that if we could elect two to five Independents to the U.S. Senate, it would break the gridlock in our federal government. The Senate is really the key chamber in terms of getting new legislation passed. President Abraham Lincoln envisioned something similar in his quest to get several new Republican senators to break the political deadlock in the 1850s.

There were already two major candidates in the South Dakota race in late 2013: former Governor Mike Rounds, the Republican frontrunner, and Rick Weiland, an aide to former Senator Tom Daschle. Both are fine men, and both had the political party machines backing them, but they were also trapped by their parties' special interests. In contrast, I had a fan base and name recognition in the state, but neither money nor any backing from a political party. I needed a boost.

And then, two events happened almost providentially. First, in 2013 a highly publicized new movie about the ABSCAM bribery scandal began to get traction. *American Hustle* featured many of Hollywood's leading actors and actresses, it was nominated for ten Academy Awards, and its popularity generated a blizzard of publicity and renewed interest in ABSCAM—and that included renewed interest in me. I was inundated with national media requests, as I had been cited as a "hero" for doing the right thing during that scandal. The result was that it reintroduced me to the public—on a national scale.

Second, the largest nationwide Native American newspaper, the *Native Sun News*, surprised me with a front- page article and photo. The headline read: "Pressler explores run for the Senate." This highly favorable article virtually announced me as a candidate. I wasn't quite ready to announce then. It got people talking and it got me moving!

Because the paper was nationwide, my old friends from all over the country read the article. They all urged me to run.

The stakes could not have been higher nationally—this made my candidacy even bolder and more challenging.

There were already two Independents in the Senate. If there were up to three to four Independents in the Senate, we could create a centrist voting "bloc" that could be the deciding faction in a closely divided Senate. In other words, we could form our own "mini caucus" to challenge the Republican and Democratic caucuses on any legislation. We could be the voice of reason and moderation in a world full of extremist voices. We could decide with whom to vote and align without worrying about Republican or Democratic backlash. Theoretically, we also could have picked the majority leader in a closely divided Senate. We could have made a real difference, and created historic change. I wanted to help make that change, and that's a large part of the reason that I ran in 2014.

I was confident that I could have won the five-way Republican primary because at that point it appeared the primary would be won by about 35 percent of the vote—and many of my advisers felt I could win. I also wanted to run for office so I could make a major contribution again. But I knew that winning the Republican primary, and subsequently the general election, would mean going back to Washington to join a traditional caucus and become part of the problem again. Even if—by some accident—I were appointed to the job as a traditional Republican, I would not accept it. I wanted my old Senate seat, but I wanted the freedom to serve the people of South Dakota and the nation without being beholden to either political party's demands, or agendas, or donors. As an Independent, I could work with both sides and with the president to gain fair treatment for South Dakota. I wanted to play both sides from the middle.

I am a "moderate centrist": I believe in gradual steps to get things done and I believe in compromise to solve real problems. So, I decided to run an old-fashioned campaign— one that focused on the critical issues facing South Dakota and the nation, not one that bashed my opponents. I wanted this experimental, idealistic, and innovative campaign to be low budget, with only positive ads and positive messaging and no response to negative campaigning. In debates, campaign events, and media interviews, I decided I would just address the issues and pretty much ignore any personal matters. And, if elected, I promised I would serve only one, six-year term, so I could focus my time in office on serving the people of South Dakota, not on raising money for my next campaign.

Any senator, even if you are serving for only one term, has to assume many fundraising responsibilities for your caucus. Both parties have "caucuses," factions that work together to pursue their interests through the legislative process. In the U.S. House and Senate, they are very partisan and very powerful. Indeed, party leadership currently recommends spending four hours per day on fundraising. While the real issue is certainly how much influence this excessive fundraising has, it also takes valuable time away from the business of legislating.

The spiritual side of me also inspired my candidacy and my desire to do something for the "public good." From my days of being taught by service-oriented nuns in Humboldt, South Dakota, to attending a variety of churches over the years, and to my present-day membership in the Church of Jesus Christ of Latter-day Saints, I have always kept service to God as my main goal. To me, that means service to my fellow man.

To most people, my goals were too idealistic, maybe even naïve. But I had at last arrived at a point in my life where I was going to speak out freely. Having that freedom as a United States senator would make it one of the best jobs in the world. The way it currently is constituted, a United States Senate seat comes with such demanding fundraising requirements that it frequently turns out to be the worst job in the world for many idealistic people. I set out to change that with my 2014 campaign.

CHAPTER 2

The Day That Changed Everything

O ctober 8, 2014. Four more weeks of hard campaigning were ahead of me before the South Dakota voters would head to the polls. They would be deciding if they would send me back to the U.S. Senate after more than eighteen years out of office.

On that morning, I awoke at my usual hour (early) and made plans to continue my daily campaign routine: get out and talk to as many voters as possible. This was not an easy task. Running as an Independent—without an army of campaign staffers, volunteers, and surrogate speakers— meant I had to rely on my handshakes alone.

Every day for the last twelve months, I had been telling hundreds of people *in person* that I was running as an Independent to bring a moderate voice to the Senate—one who would work with *both* political parties. Every day, I had been telling them that I would not be beholden to anyone while in office, as I would not raise any money and I would only serve one term. Every day, I reiterated my pledge to them to break the poisonous, partisan gridlock choking our country, by serving as an Independent.

I had a good feeling about our campaign. In our travels around the state, we were hearing a lot of encouraging words from longtime supporters as well as total strangers—of all ages! Based on my past campaign experience, things felt like they were coming together. It was pure instinct, but I was right.

Until that morning in October, the reaction to my campaign among the political party operatives had been rather dismissive. Even though I was steadily ascending in the polls, some were still calling me a political spoiler. The media in South Dakota was covering my campaign, but none thought that I had a really serious chance to upset the political establishment. And the national media still viewed me as an election-year curiosity.

But that October day changed everything and probably secured my footnote in political campaign history!

That day, three major media outlets in my state published the results of a statewide poll: "Survey South Dakota—conducted by Survey USA on behalf of the *Aberdeen American News*, KSFY-TV of Sioux Falls and KOTA-TV of Rapid City—was of 616 likely voters and was conducted between Oct. 1 and [October 5]." The poll showed me tied for the lead and was the first indication that I had a real shot at winning this race! This little experiment I was running as an Independent was working!

Nate Silver, the nation's leading political statistician who has a blog called *FiveThirtyEight.com*, noticed the survey immediately. Silver accurately predicted the winner of forty- nine of the fifty states in the 2008 presidential elections. In 2012, he once again correctly predicted the winner of all fifty states and the District of Columbia, plus thirty-one of thirty- three of the Senate races. Political media pay attention to him.

In his blog post late in the evening of October 7, he said, "This is a challenging race to forecast—both because of the inconsistent polling and the three-way dynamic. But the logic programmed into the *FiveThirtyEight* model is as follows: because Pressler is more ideologically similar to Rounds than Weiland—at least according to the statistical measures that we use—the model assumes that Pressler and Rounds will mostly trade votes with one another rather than with Weiland. In other words, Pressler's gains will tend to come at Rounds' expense, and vice versa. That makes Pressler the more likely candidate to pull off the upset; he can gain ground relative to the frontrunner more quickly."

South Dakota readers woke up to this poll and the national media woke up to Silver's blog. When I read it, I couldn't believe it and was a bit tongue-tied for a few hours. The phones started to explode. Calls were coming in from supporters, national media, volunteers, international media, and vendors. Everyone was offering support, but without a large and paid staff, we couldn't "harvest" all this generosity. In other words, my tiny volunteer staff didn't have the bandwidth to follow up and manage the offers to help. It was a nice problem to have, but it was hard to keep up with the demand for my time. We weren't ready for this kind of onslaught.

I gave numerous media interviews over the course of the next few days and the resulting headlines were telling. *The Washington Post* said, "A surprise in the South Dakota race?" *The Atlantic Monthly* wrote, "The Rise of the Independents?" That Sunday, *The New York Times* ran a front-page story that read, "Senate Contest in South Dakota Is Free-for-All." *Vice* led with "South Dakota's Larry Pressler Is the Most Interesting Candidate of 2014." *The National Journal* said enthusiastically, "The Improbable Career of Cowboy Poetry Aficionado, Senate Candidate Larry Pressler."

Most of these national publications focused on the implications of a Pressler victory on the balance of power in the Senate. With whom would I caucus, *The Washington Post* mused? In an article published online in the *Post* on October 8, liberal blogger Greg Sargent wistfully wrote, "It's not impossible that Pressler could win and decline to caucus with the Republicans, or that Pressler's presence could somehow throw victory to Dem Rick Weiland."

Sargent went on:

But this creates a difficult situation for Democrats. Some Dems seem to believe that, if there is any chance of beating Rounds, the more likely way is for Pressler to win. This creates an incentive for Dems to want Weiland to drop out, thus making a Pressler win more likely. The mere chance that Pressler might caucus with Dems makes this an outcome they want; even barring that, the prospect of Pressler forcing national Republicans to sink more resources into this race for their candidate is also very inviting to Democrats. But, at the same time, top Dems are loath to root against the Democratic candidate, and there is the possibility of divisions within the party over this.

The New York Times published a front-page story on my campaign in October and it included this photo. Ryan Henriksen/The New York Times/Redux.

The Atlantic Monthly said in an online article also published on October 8, "The self-financed independent in Kansas, Greg Orman, has built a steady lead in his race against longtime GOP incumbent Senator Pat Roberts, while a new poll out Wednesday showed another unaligned hopeful, former Senator Larry Pressler, ascending in South Dakota. The surprising strength of Orman and Pressler raises the possibility that the Senate will have more members who were not elected on a party ticket than it has had in more than a century." It now seemed my campaign (and that of Greg Orman's in Kansas) could create an historic precedent.

In other words, my potential election to the U.S. Senate in 2014 had major, national implications. In those heady days in early October when I was leading in the polls, several political scientists and historians called me to discuss my candidacy. They felt that we were on the verge of something new and big in the United States. Why? Because if the nation could elect four Independents to the Senate that year, the Independent senators could create our own, albeit small, Independent caucus.

With forty-eight Republicans and forty-eight Democrats in the Senate, we four Independents could have been the tiebreakers on any highly divisive issue. Theoretically, we could have controlled the leadership outcome and voted to elect Maine Senator Angus King the Senate Majority Leader. For example, if there had been a forty-eight-Republican/ forty-eight-Democratic split with four Independents, the Independents could have formed a caucus and controlled the leadership outcome. Our small but powerful Independent caucus could have indeed started a "third way."

It felt like we were on the verge of something very big, and we were.

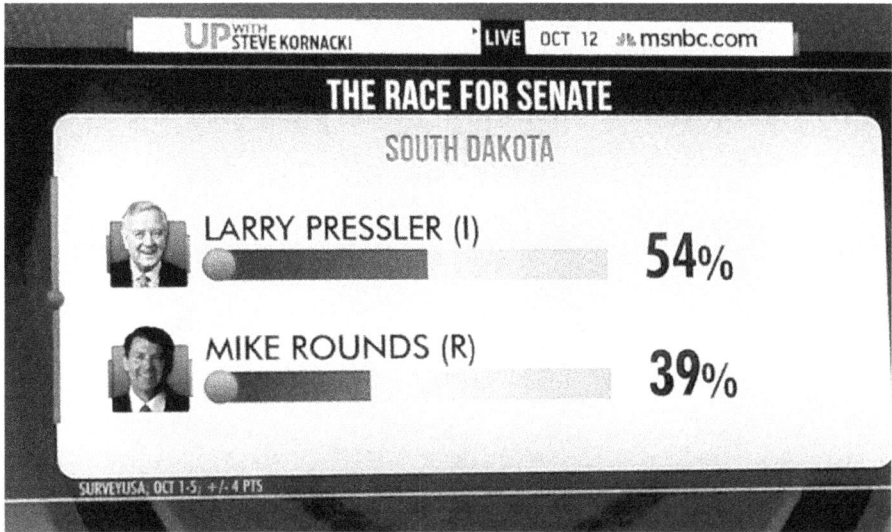

This poll appeared on MSNBC's Up with Steve Kornacki show. Photo – Larry Pressler.

CHAPTER 3

The Roots of My Independence

To understand how I got to the national stage and why I ran for the Senate as an Independent in 2014, it is important to understand where I started. People who knew me when I was growing up in South Dakota were frankly amazed that I ended up as a United States senator for three terms. They remembered a painfully shy farm boy with a cowlick and a severe stammer who found it hard to look people in the eye. And they remembered right.

If the circumstances of one's birth and DNA were all there were to human destiny—a proposition, I don't subscribe to for a minute—I would have followed in my father's footsteps and become a farmer. Farming is an honorable occupation and a self-fulfilling way of life. But farming wasn't to be my fate. Instead, through a series of twists and turns, luck, my own innate abilities, and what I believe was the intervention of God, I became, in Theodore Roosevelt's famous phrase, "a man in the arena."

When I was born, on March 29, 1942, and christened Lawrence Lee after my uncle, Lawrence Douvier, there was nothing in the stars that marked me for "the arena." My family scratched out a bare existence on a rented quarter section, 160 hardscrabble acres, in Grand Meadow Township in Minnehaha County. We lived twenty-two miles southwest of Sioux Falls, the state's largest city, which is named for the picturesque Big Sioux River rapids that run through town. But we might as well have lived on the edge of the American frontier in a previous century.

Providing for a large family on a rented quarter section is an exceedingly hazardous existence. Forty percent of everything you earn goes to the landlord. In addition to the vagaries of the weather, a year-to-year renter never knows when the landlord might take it into his head to throw you off his property and consign you and your family to a life of abject poverty. For the first several years of my life, I lived in a home with no electricity, no running water, and no plumbing. Seven of us—my father, my mother, my four siblings, and I shared a wooden outhouse known as a "two-holer" because it allowed two people to use the facility at the same time.

I remember the cattle in our barnyard with ice crystals on their eyelashes, standing through the South Dakota winter knee-deep in snowdrifts taller than myself. In the spring we placed salt blocks on a wooden trough. The cattle licked it until it was gone, and then continued licking the empty boards for days afterward—so like our own rough-grained life. I remember the day we got electricity, the moment I turned on a light switch for the first time. Electric power, when the Rural Electric Association (REA) came after World War II, made it possible to have a water pump, which in turn ended the need for my mother and three sisters to haul water in buckets to the house.

We were a devoutly Catholic family, attending church every week and praying the rosary every night together. Despite not being very warm and always very reserved in front of us, my parents instilled in us a strong work ethic, sense of frugality, honesty, and spirituality. From them, I learned right from wrong. In those days, many farmers got away with turning in less corn from their federally subsidized storage bins than they had been paid for. The practice was called skimming. A farmer could pocket a few hundred dollars by skimming a couple of hundred bushels of corn. Dad was scrupulous about turning in the exact amount.

One time as I was helping him build a small granary in which to store government corn, he said, "I expect the government to be honest with me, as it always has been. I think the money we pay them goes for good purposes, so I'm careful to be honest with the government."

My mother set a good example as well. Once, after shopping, Mother realized that she'd been given too much change, so she marched back into the store and returned the extra dollars. The clerk seemed more annoyed than grateful, but Mother didn't mind. She didn't expect to be patted on the back for doing the right thing. Her example was instilled in us. She always naturally did the ethical thing.

As a result of my family's poverty, and the terrible insecurity that goes with being poor, I know what it feels like to be afflicted with a sense of self-doubt and low self-esteem. I also know what it feels like to desperately want to overcome your low status in life and better yourself. These are feelings that you never completely get over. All of this may help explain two apparently contradictory sides of my personality: a bashfulness that makes me acutely self-conscious and reluctant to draw attention to myself, and—at the same time—a burning desire to be of service to others and to achieve great things.

I first became aware of my stammer when I was three or four years old. Sometimes when I stumbled over a word, my father would say, "Larry, just spit it out!" Dad didn't mean to be cruel, but I don't think he ever identified with me the way he did with my younger brother Dan. Maybe it was because I was a cerebral kid and that made my father uncomfortable. In any case, no one in the family ever made fun of me because of the stammer. But my speech impediment aggravated my natural shyness and, for many years, it made me reluctant to speak in public—definitely not an attribute you normally associate with a future politician.

At the age of ten or eleven, a neighbor, Elmer Anderson,

took me under his wing. He led the local chapter of 4-H, a national agricultural youth organization administered by the U.S. Department of Agriculture. Through 4-H, we were taught that family-farm life was the best life in America, and that farming was a noble profession. As the first Catholic invited to join the local 4-H chapter, the Humboldt Hustlers, I felt very self-conscious. Mr. Anderson, our chapter leader, disdained the religious divisions that then existed in our community. Catholics shopped at the Catholic grocery store, Protestants at the Protestant grocery store. By including me in the club, he made a courageous statement.

Joining 4-H opened a whole new world to me. No longer defined by the circumstances of my birth, economic status, or religion, I was instead judged by what I could accomplish in my own right. It built my self-confidence to travel to county and state fairs, where major breeders showed their best hogs and cattle. My dad cosigned a note for me at the Community Bank of Humboldt for $125. I used the money to build a small pig house called a farrowing crate. My first sow, Sally, a purebred Spotted Poland-China pig, gave birth to eight piglets—five boars and three gilts. Sadly, Sally accidentally lay on one of them and killed it—so I only weaned seven live piglets from her. Subsequently, one of the boars won first prize at the Sioux Empire Fair, and later at the South Dakota State Fair in Huron. My 4-H career was launched!

After I entered Humboldt High School, I tried some 4-H public speaking. My first public demonstration was titled, "How to Make a Rope Halter," which I managed to deliver without too much stammering. I received an enthusiastic round of applause from my fellow 4-Hers.

My growing knowledge and self-confidence were starting to make waves at home. Dad's withdrawn and introverted personality was reflected in his approach to farming. As I grew older, his old-fashioned ideas grated on me. I was getting straight As in school, and teachers were saying, "Larry has the brains to be something big." I began arguing with Dad at the dinner table, which caused a lot of tension. I wanted him to follow the example of several of our neighbors who had milking machines and raised purebred livestock instead of grade livestock. But Dad stuck with his livestock and his inexpensive tractor, a two-plow VAC Case without a cab, which meant that when he worked in the field, he was exposed to the elements. He didn't even have an umbrella to protect himself from the sun in the brutal South Dakota summers.

Dad had a basic farming strategy and he stuck with it, just like his father had. He focused on low-capital (and low-risk) investments and old-fashioned farming. He wasn't interested in the newest techniques or technology or expanding his farm. He knew what worked for him. He fed his family, paid all his bills, eventually bought his farm, and left enough money to care for his widow after he died, so I can't fault him for his resistance. Call it a generational divide or just my own form of rebellion.

Years later, I became friends with my fellow Rhodes Scholar and Harvard Business School professor Clayton Christensen, who coined the term "disruptive innovation." By his definition, a disruptive innovation is one that helps create a new market and eventually disrupts an existing market, displacing an earlier technology. In part, 4-H was created to do just this type of disruption. The Department of Agriculture wanted to educate America's farmers about new farming technology and products, in hopes that the younger generation would introduce them to their families. Without knowing it, I was trying to be a positive disrupter—but my dad saw it as interference. That contributed to our discomfort with each other.

I never particularly thought of myself as a bright student. But I worked very hard, both in school and after school. I hired myself out to neighboring farmers for the then- standard one dollar per hour. In the winter months, I pitched manure and cleaned out silos. On weekends, I tended to my 4-H livestock. I don't want to leave the impression that all was doom and drudgery in my South Dakota high school in the 1950s. Despite my family's poverty and my stammer, I had a pretty positive outlook on life. I used to dream about traveling to exotic places, like India, and becoming somebody important who would help others. I'd get books from the state library, which had a free-mailing system, and I read as much as I could about foreign countries. Having access to more books than any small-town library could house opened up my mind to the vast world out there beyond Humboldt.

It was during this time that I first read about the Hindu religion, the Book of Mormon, the Koran and, of course, the Bible. We did not emphasize reading the Bible very much in the Roman Catholic Church in those days. The nuns and our local priest became rather nervous at how many other faiths' religious texts I was reading! But it gave me a chance to develop my own sense of spirituality. During this period, I also read about Confucianism and decided that this philosophy—based on kindness, mutual respect, and an appreciation of character—might be the best way to serve mankind.

Despite the challenges I faced growing up poor and my severe stuttering, I was fortunate to have some great mentors, and I was determined to go to college. I still remember the strange mix of joy, wonderment, spiritual movement, and apprehension that I felt when I set foot on the University of South Dakota's sprawling, 216-acre park- like campus in Vermillion, a picturesque town nestled along the bluffs above the Missouri River. I arrived with all my farm-boy idealism intact. It was September 1960, a watershed moment in American history and a watershed moment in my life.

CHAPTER 4

Onward to the Oval Office and Oxford as a Rhodes Scholar

The University of South Dakota (USD) is one of the best small public universities in the nation, and it boasts many distinguished alumni. Some of its famous graduates include historians, artists, businessmen, several United States senators and congressmen, *USA Today* and Gannett founder Al Neuharth, and one NBC anchor, Tom Brokaw, who was a contemporary of mine while there. As one of the first in my family to attend college, I felt blessed by God. Like other poor farm boys attending college at the time, I earned my board washing dishes and serving food. I also had a work/study job in the Government Research Bureau, where I clipped newspapers from around the state and created folders on various subjects for professors.

College opened up a whole new world for me, introducing me to a more diverse group of people and many professional mentors. One of those mentors was USD's legendary political science professor, Dr. William O. Farber. He inspired a love of public service in me and shepherded the careers of a number of male students over several decades. I took several of Doc Farber's classes. He recognized and fueled my ambitions, encouraging me to aim high. He boosted my self-confidence and offered me many new opportunities to excel and prove myself. His mantra was, "Work hard!"

In my freshman year, I became a waiter in the university's faculty dining room. On John F. Kennedy's Inauguration day, as I was serving lunch, I glanced at the television set up on the wall and saw the elderly poet Robert Frost, with his papers blowing in the cold January wind as he tried to read a verse he had written. In contrast, the youthful new president approached the podium and began delivering the most riveting speech I had ever heard. He issued a call to all Americans that resonated with me: "...Let every nation know, whether it wishes us well or ill, that we shall pay any price, bear any burden, meet any hardship, support any friend, oppose any foe to assure the survival and the success of liberty..." I was frozen on the spot. One of the dining room supervisors reprimanded me and demanded that I keep moving and clear my tables. I could not have imagined that, two years later, I would get the chance to meet the president in person.

At USD, I found my way to the school's speech clinic to attend a stammer/stutter workshop. The speech therapists there did the best they could with limited resources, but even they couldn't tell me exactly what caused my problem or exactly how to fix it. I forced myself to join the debate team because I simply refused to let my affliction get the better of me. But I still have a stammer to this day.

And, then, another blessing from God was bestowed on me—I was invited to spend the second half of my freshman year in Egypt, where I attended the International Agricultural Exhibition in Cairo as an American representative of 4-H. What a thrill for a farmer's son from the sticks of South Dakota to travel overseas. I was the first in my family to get a passport! When I returned to the university, I had to take a heavy dose of summer school courses to make up the lost credits, but the trip was worth it. My independence had ignited an international spirit.

In my junior year, I ran for president of the student body, and won the election. In March of 1963, another blessing from

God: I was thrilled to be named one of four all-American 4-Hers selected to present the "4-H Report to the Nation" to President Kennedy in the Oval Office. Standing next to President Kennedy was the most awe-inducing experience of my young life, although he paid much more attention to Fay Craig, my counterpart from Mississippi. She was really pretty with a deep Southern accent that charmed both the president and me. Kennedy, of course, was tragically assassinated a few short months later.

Fay Craig (center) and I (right) were two 4-H members—selected from 2.3 million 4-Hers from around the country—to present the "1963 4-H Report to the Nation" to President Kennedy in the White House Oval Office. Photo courtesy of the White House.

By the first semester of my senior year, I had a girlfriend. Both of us were looking forward to graduation, but we had very different futures in mind. She wanted to get married and have children; I wanted to be a Rhodes Scholar and see the world. Doc Farber had told me about this prestigious scholarship and encouraged me to submit an application. In those days, Rhodes

Scholars couldn't be engaged or married, so I broke off our relationship. I think I broke her heart. I know I broke my own.

The Rhodes Scholarship is the oldest and most celebrated international fellowship award in the country. Rhodes Scholars are chosen for their noteworthy scholarship achievements, but also for their character, commitment to others and to the common good, and for their potential for civic-minded leadership. The Rhodes Trust accepted very few candidates with my rural background from my alma mater. The odds of my winning a coveted spot in the 1964 class of scholars seemed long indeed. Professor Farber urged me not to be discouraged. He pointed out that my farm background and 4-H skills in judging purebred animals were just the kind of "manly experiences" that Cecil Rhodes required when he founded the scholarships. In the Midwest, interviews for the Rhodes scholarships were held in Chicago, and the announcement of winners was made at a formal dinner. Because of my lack of experience with proper table manners, I was scared to death that I'd make some terrible faux pas and lose out.

Luckily, I was seated across the table from an elegant Episcopal bishop from Chicago who was on the selection committee. I watched him handling his eating utensils and imitated his selection from the confusing array of forks, knives, spoons, and glasses. And then, in the middle of dinner, I heard my name being announced as a Rhodes Scholar. In the course of four years, I had traveled from a farmhouse in South Dakota to acceptance at Oxford University. It was an unlikely journey, but just the type of challenge I have pursued throughout my life. The 2014 campaign was no exception.

In September 1964, I was one of thirty-two American Rhodes Scholars and about one hundred additional American graduate students who boarded the S.S. *France* in New York Harbor and set sail for Southampton, England. Despite several days of rough seas, the trip was an exhilarating adventure. There I was, in the middle of the Atlantic Ocean, engaging in intellectually stimulating bull sessions with a bunch of brilliant young men from all over America. Most of the conversations were about the Vietnam War draft. Before leaving for England, all of us had been required to go to our local draft boards and obtain a document called Permission to Leave the Country, which had to be renewed each year. If you had a fair amount of money and the brains to stay in graduate school, or if your parents hobnobbed with the members of the establishment or had political clout with the local draft board, you could avoid conscription until age of twenty-six, when you were no longer eligible to be drafted. Another popular way of avoiding the draft at that time was to find a doctor who was willing to sign a letter saying you had some physical or emotional disability that made you ineligible to serve in the military.

Along with the topic of the draft, there were fierce debates aboard the *S.S. France* about the 1964 presidential race, which pitted President Lyndon Johnson, a New Deal liberal, against Senator Barry Goldwater, a dyed-in-the-wool conservative. Many of the Rhodes Scholars came from liberal schools and had been sponsored by left-leaning professors.

These young men opposed Johnson's escalation in Vietnam, but they hated Barry Goldwater even more than the war. As a result, almost all of them were reluctant supporters of the president. I also felt that many of the European-bound students were mouthing leftist platitudes and giving the anti- Communist Goldwater a bum rap.

At the time, my beliefs on the Vietnam War were mixed. On the one hand, I believed Presidents Kennedy and Johnson when they said that America had to stand and fight for democracy in Vietnam. On the other hand, I had some doubts about Secretary of Defense Robert McNamara's reports of progress. Much later in my life, when I heard the White House tapes, I realized that the American public was being deceived, especially by President Johnson.

What bothered me the most was that almost all of the 130 young Americans on board bound for study in Europe seemed to be scheming to avoid military service. In my view, whether you agreed with the war or not, you had a duty to answer your country's call to serve. So I often found myself the odd man out, defending Barry Goldwater and Lyndon Johnson—and I only partially agreed with both men.

When we landed in Southampton, E.T. Williams, the Warden of Rhodes House (or the Rodent of Wards House, as he was humorously referred to behind his back), met us at the pier with a lorry, a truck designed to carry troops. The bumpy hour-and-twenty-minute ride to Oxford, the oldest university in the English-speaking world, was a lot rougher than some of our days at sea. As we approached Oxford, I saw the medieval spires, which looked like something out of a fairy tale. Then I was assigned to St. Edmund Hall, a college distinguished for its rowing prowess and undistinguished for its comfort, and discovered that student housing hadn't improved much in the several centuries since Oxford's founding. The rooms were monkishly bare. There was no central heating. And if you wanted to go to the bathroom or bathe, you had to brave frigid morning temperatures and carry your clothes to a different building, where there were some rudimentary stalls and showers and not much hot water. Funnily enough, there were more plumbing "luxuries" back on my family farm than in St. Edmund's Hall, all of which compounded my feelings of loneliness and homesickness.

By the time of my arrival in Oxford, student demonstrations against the United States had begun, and the depth of hatred for America distressed me. I was even more upset by the behavior of some of my fellow Americans (including the

Rhodes Scholars), who wholeheartedly joined in the hate-America binge. In our conversations, I came to the conclusion that what they really wanted to avoid was anything that might interrupt the upward trajectory of their privileged careers—and that included military service. Had they come to Oxford to further their education and prepare themselves for a life of public service—as the Rhodes Scholarship founder envisioned for the scholarship's recipients? Or were they at Oxford to escape the draft and feather their own nests? I found it impossible to have a rational discussion with anyone wrapped in a cloak of self- righteous indignation about America's "immoral" and "wicked" foreign policy. As a result, I came to question the motives of some of my fellow American students at Oxford.

Looking back, I believe that the ferocious battles that raged over the Vietnam War draft—battles that seemed magnified in the setting of a foreign university—created a fracture in the American psyche that has never healed. At least it's never completely healed in my own psyche.

Those battles often pitted the privileged elite, who found a multitude of ways to dodge the draft, against the less advantaged, who accounted for most of the 58,220 American dead in Vietnam. The fissures between the affluent and non-affluent, between the educated and less well educated, between whites and blacks, between the powerful and powerless—these fissures were fundamentally inconsistent with America's democratic traditions. In my opinion, they marked the beginning of America's ethical decline.

The elite of my generation argued that because the Vietnam War was "immoral," it was honorable of them to resist the draft. In other words, they justified their decision on idealistic grounds— a "noble" lie! This was an unconscious rationalization at best, and a complete cop-out at worst.

While they pursued their accelerated careers and rose to

become the leaders in their professions, others who were less well connected and less affluent went to Vietnam in their place. In short, with a tragic flaw in their reasoning—a dishonest and distorted sense of values—this dishonesty infected an entire generation. I had respect for the very small number who were honest enough to say, "I just plain don't want to serve." At least they admitted their true motivations. History has proved my suspicions. As soon as the draft was eliminated and the all-volunteer service was instituted, most of the antiwar movement vanished.

The Rhodes Scholarship program usually runs for two years. As I thought about my situation in Oxford, it occurred to me that for every person, like me, who won a draft deferment or a cozy spot in a noncombatant National Guard unit, someone poorer or less educated—often an African American or Hispanic or Native American—had to serve.

Thus the question for me was: *what was the right thing to do? I had to confront the very basis of my idealism.*

CHAPTER 5

Invisible Wounds from Vietnam

Sitting on my safe perch as a Rhodes Scholar at Oxford, I watched the Vietnam War continue to rage on. I knew that I could probably prolong my student deferment and perhaps even stretch it out to the age of twenty-six, when I'd no longer be liable for the draft. But when I thought that way, I also thought of something my father had told me just before I left for Oxford. "If you decide not to go to Vietnam," Dad said, "it will mean that someone poorer and less able than you will have to go in your place. And knowing you, that will trouble your conscience for the rest of your life. So you might as well just go and do it."

My father thought it would be a glorious thing if I became an Army officer. He had not served in World War II because farmers were compelled to stay and farm to alleviate the food shortage. The country needed its farmers during World War II, but my dad always regretted his lack of service. "You mean," he said in an incredulous tone, "that you have a chance to become an officer in the United States Army and that you're actually thinking of turning it down? My God, son, you'll be the first officer in our family!"

In my father's eyes, being an Army officer was worth a lot more than being a Rhodes Scholar. And despite our dinner table debates over farming methods, and the divergent paths our lives had taken, I was no different from most sons. I longed to win my father's approval.

And so I told the Warden of Rhodes House, E.T. Williams, that I was going to give up my draft exemption and join the Army. Williams, who had served in World War II in the British Army, was delighted. "Wonderful!" he said. "You are the first and only Rhodes Scholar who has been willing to volunteer for Vietnam. I see a steady stream of them with complex plans to avoid the draft. If that's what you want to do, I'll support you. Go and do the Vietnam military thing, and if you want to, you can come back to Oxford and do the second year at some future time. Whatever you decide, you will always be a Rhodes Scholar in good standing." My decision to join the military meant that I had to prepare for my diploma in public administration after only one year at Oxford. And that, in turn, meant I had to spend every waking hour in the Radcliffe Camera, an eighteenth-century architectural wonder that holds some 600,000 books and is the main reading room of the Bodleian Library, Oxford's main library.

Because of a childhood farm accident, when a heavy grain auger fell on me, I suffered from chronic back problems and almost didn't pass the Army's physical exam. You might say that this stammerer had to talk his way into uniform! That uniform was a big hit when I returned home to Humboldt after four months of basic training at Fort Benjamin Harrison in Indiana. I stood six-foot-three and weighed 165 pounds, and I must have looked like a scarecrow in my freshly pressed second lieutenant's uniform. But my mother was so proud that she insisted I go around and visit all my relatives.

As a newly minted Army lieutenant, I was shipped off to Vietnam and posted on the outskirts of Cân Thó, the capital of Dinh Tuong Province and the largest city in the Mekong Delta, the rice basket of Vietnam. My unit's job was to provide military security along Highway 4 for the vital food supplies moving from the rice paddies and vegetable farms in the Delta to the capital city of Saigon. Our encampment at Cân Thó was surrounded by a deep defensive trench, which had been cleared of all trees by Agent Orange, the code name for the herbicides and defoliants used by the U.S. military. It was later discovered that Agent Orange contained an extremely toxic dioxin compound that caused birth defects, mental disabilities, skin and respiratory disorders, and cancers. Years later, I tried unsuccessfully to get legislation passed that would have funded Agent Orange research.

The Viet Cong (or "VC"), the Communist-led guerilla force supported by North Vietnam, controlled the countryside at night, so we had to run our food convoys during the daytime. A lot of Vietnamese were reluctant to drive for us, because we came under sniper fire from the VC. American troops ended up doing most of the driving. The snipers liked shooting at the truck drivers, but they liked targeting American officers even more. I was always armed, but I still felt like a sitting duck. It was dangerous duty.

On the way back to the Delta from Saigon, we transported supplies, farm equipment, and small motor pumps. We distributed the pumps to farmers who were loyal to our cause. They were used for many things, including running small boats through the canals to transport goods and irrigation. Farmers had to "prove" they weren't VC to get one.

Drawing on the economics expertise I had acquired at Oxford, I wrote a four-page report called "The Distribution of Motor Pumps in Dinh Tuong Province." It was sent up the chain of command and was influential enough to get me transferred to the Military Assistance Command Vietnam (MACV) pacification program at Army headquarters in Saigon to produce more of these types of reports. I soon realized that I had stumbled into the midst of a bitter debate between members of the State Department—who argued that the war was going badly—and the Pentagon, who argued just as vociferously that we were making progress.

One of the chief items in dispute was the amount of rice and produce that was getting through the roadblocks set up by the VC.

On my own initiative, I went out and counted the number of vegetable trucks that were making it from Dalat, a city in the Central Highlands north of Saigon. In my subsequent report, I noted that Vietnamese farmers had learned how to bribe their way through the VC roadblocks, and that as a result, there was as much food reaching Saigon as there had been the year before. As a reward, I was sent to Dalat, where I did a series of interviews with vegetable truckers. In my subsequent memo, titled "Ruckus in a Radish Patch," I reported that, contrary to what the doomsayers in the State Department were saying, essential foodstuffs were in fact getting through to Saigon—a conclusion that added to my unpopularity among the Foreign Service types.

In late 1967, I contracted hepatitis and was sent to a military convalescent center in South Vietnam. I experienced frightening nightmares when I was there. The events that triggered these nightmares had taken place earlier that year. At the time, the American news media were up in arms about the U.S. military's accounting of enemy body counts, which the journalists charged were flagrantly inflated. To counter their negative stories, the South Vietnamese government instituted a body count verification program to verify the statistics. Teams of Vietnamese soldiers and some American advisers were dispatched into the field to provide eyewitness accounts. I accompanied one of these teams. What I saw during that mission was seared forever in my mind's eye: dozens of dead Vietnamese (it was impossible to tell whether they were VC or civilians), their brains spilling out of their broken skulls, their teeth scattered on the blood-soaked ground. And worse—much, much worse.

The sights that met me at the convalescent center were just as horrific as those on fields of old battles. I saw soldiers and Marines with empty eye sockets and half their faces blown away. Some of the men were in such horrible condition that they were kept strapped down and in induced comas until they could be evacuated to better-equipped military hospitals in Japan and the Philippines.

All of these encounters have resulted in my having flashbacks, which plague me to this day. I'd always thought that I must have been somewhat squeamish to feel such horror. But I have learned that these feelings are a natural human reaction in men who go to war.

Spurred by producer Ken Burns' PBS documentary series on the Civil War, I read an editorial in *The New York Times* called "The Dead of Antietam." The article, written in 1862, described the impact of a photography exhibit on the aftermath of the Battle of Antietam, which was on display in New York City at the time. The photographs of dead bodies and the battle scene, taken and assembled by famous Civil War photographer Mathew Brady, were some of the most graphic war images ever displayed to the public—and they in part triggered anti-draft riots against President Lincoln in New York City. Visitors were shocked. It justified my own horrific feelings.

Although I didn't know it then, I was suffering from post-traumatic stress disorder (PTSD), an anxiety condition that used to be called battle fatigue or shell shock. While I was in Vietnam, the Army awarded me a total of fifteen medals, including the Bronze Star and the Army Commendation Medal. Once, as we were making a helicopter landing with Vietnamese forces in the Delta, several mortars detonated and my left hand was slightly injured. We were also under some sniper fire. The commander, an Army colonel, wanted to submit me for a Purple Heart medal.

Suffering a wound under enemy fire is the requirement for a Purple Heart. The colonel said I qualified. But I declined because I had seen severely wounded soldiers who really deserved a Purple Heart and never received one. In a document the colonel wrote at the time, he said, "One visit was to an extremely dangerous area... I afforded those officers who did not wish to continue [the chance] to drop out and about 40% did. Larry Pressler chose to continue the mission, for which he had volunteered... Larry was eligible for an award for that mission, but his modesty precluded his accepting any."

Wearing the Purple Heart for the rest of my life would have felt disingenuous. I saw the awarding of medals as haphazard; it depended entirely on who wrote you up and how much you pushed to be recognized. Also, I had seen men injured by friendly fire and they did not receive the Purple Heart. I was turned off by the whole system.

As a lieutenant in the U.S. Army in Vietnam in 1967–1968, I found wearing a helmet in the Delta heat and humidity miserable! Photo courtesy of the U.S. Army.

More fundamentally, I had become turned off by the whole war. My rejection of the Purple Heart on that day was a turning point in my feelings about the war and my feelings about life. From that point on, I never totally trusted government authority again and this incident is probably the root of my independence. Until the Tet Offensive in early 1968, I thought we were winning the "hearts and minds" of the Vietnamese people. I was young and idealistic enough that I had actually believed President Johnson and Secretary of Defense McNamara that we were winning this war. I thought we were making a difference—trying our best to help the Vietnamese build a democracy. Obviously, we were not. The Tet Offensive proved that our government's leaders had been lying to the troops *and to me.* The VC had control of the entire countryside and the loyalty of the common Vietnamese. Our allies and we were only in control of a few cities. It became very apparent that our economic development activities were not making an iota of difference. The people just viewed us as occupiers. I came to the conclusion that many others have reached: that we cannot use ground forces or "boots on the ground" for nation-building efforts. Our war in Iraq proved that point once again.

In 1974, I became one of the first Vietnam combat veterans to be elected to Congress. As the years wore on, and the rancor and acrimony over the Vietnam War receded in memory, my military service was no longer seen as something shameful. In fact, it bestowed on me a certain aura. Some of the very people who had heaped scorn on those who served in Vietnam began referring to us as valiant, even heroic. But after seeing the horrors of war—and the amazing bravery of so many ordinary Americans—I felt that I was an improbable hero, and I looked for an opportunity to say so. The chance came one day when my fellow senator and Vietnam veteran John Kerry announced in a meeting, "I am joined by a genuine hero of the Vietnam War, Larry Pressler." I jumped out of my chair and, in a stammer-free voice, proclaimed: "No, not a hero, not a hero. I just did my job." I considered it part of my civic duty.

While still in Vietnam, I took the LSAT, the law school admission test, and I received word that my scores were good enough to earn me a place at Harvard Law School. In the summer of 1968, I returned to the States, where I separated from the military at the old Oakland Army Base in the San Francisco Bay area. I distinctly recall being advised not to wear my uniform in San Francisco, as I would likely be spit on or accosted. Once again a civilian, I set off across the country in a used Volkswagen Beetle for Harvard Law School.

During my years at Harvard Law, from 1968 to 1971, the place was a hotbed of resistance to the Vietnam War. Students published dozens of leaflets on how to avoid the draft; they burned their draft cards, held sit-ins, boycotted classes, and organized nonstop demonstrations. There was a drinking/marijuana culture associated with student life that I didn't like. I was working part-time, and intensely busy with my studies. We had classes six days a week.

I was one of the very few Vietnam veterans in my class of 550 law students. My service in Vietnam was a black mark against me, and some of the more radical students viewed me as an accomplice to a crime. Even the faculty exhibited some hostility, as some joined their students in antiwar protests. They all assumed that I was pro-war because I had served, while in reality I had come to believe that Vietnam was a lost cause. My experience had also made me very reticent regarding committing ground troops in foreign conflicts. In short, my service in Vietnam had seared my soul and instilled in me a feeling of responsibility to ensure our nation never again engaged in a needless foreign war. It was another reason I ran in 2014.

The quality of the education I was receiving at Harvard Law School was top-notch. Upon graduation, I was offered a job at

Cravath, Swaine & Moore, the second oldest law firm in America and one of the most prestigious in the world. Although tempted to accept it—a career with a top law firm like Cravath could be very financially lucrative, and I was in debt—I turned it down.

Instead I opted for a much lower-paying public service job as a Foreign Service Officer with the State Department. Once again the Catholic school nuns' advice, the urging from my University of South Dakota professors, and my dad's encouraging me to serve in the military all led me to pursue a career in public service. And although I had left Vietnam disillusioned, convinced that it was foolhardy for the United States to intervene militarily in unfamiliar, far-off lands, I still believed that America had a moral duty to help developing countries provide a decent life for their people.

Soon after I was mustered into the State Department, I was sent to Switzerland to work on negotiations regarding the General Agreement on Tariffs and Trade (GATT). For the next couple of years, I shuttled between Geneva and Washington, playing a small part in deciphering the intricacies of global trade. Quite frankly, the work wasn't that demanding or interesting.

And so, in the spring of 1974, I made an audacious decision that was fraught with risk, but one I felt a calling to do. Against the advice of friends and family—and with no experience in electoral politics, no organization, no support from the state Republican Party, and practically no money, I resigned from my stable job in the Foreign Service, cashed in my retirement fund and my small savings account, and moved back to South Dakota to launch a campaign for the U.S. House of Representatives from my mother's kitchen.

CHAPTER 6

From Improbable to Possible: Getting Elected to the House in 1974

W hen I arrived home in the farming community of Humboldt in 1974 to begin the race for South Dakota's First Congressional District, I was thirty-two years old. People asked me, "Why don't you run for the state legislature?" or, "Why don't you wait a few years?" What they really meant to say was, "Have you completely lost your mind?" Ironically, these were some of the same questions I received when I made the decision to run in 2014. So what made me do it?

A few weeks before, a grand jury had named President Richard Nixon as an unindicted coconspirator in the Watergate cover-up. Watching the whole scandal unfold from my comfortable State Department perch, I was disgusted by the whole sordid Watergate mess. Although I had no political connections at the time, I had met President Nixon on a social basis on a number of occasions because his daughter Tricia had married my close friend and Harvard Law School classmate, Edward Cox. I had attended the engagement party and served as a groomsman at their wedding in 1971. I admired Nixon for his brilliant foreign policy, especially his opening to China. But now, in the wake of Watergate, I thought it would be best for the country—and his family—if the seriously compromised president resigned. I felt that it was time for people of good will to band together and help clean up Washington.

Although I gave myself only a slim chance of winning a seat in the House, I thought it would be worth the effort if I could inject new ideas into the campaign and do something to help my country—just as I aspired to do again in 2014. In 1974 my platform was based on five reform principles. I also had one-page issue statements on everything from small business, to helping family farmers, senior citizens, and education, among others. I made clear that I was strongly for free trade legislation, something that was controversial with the powerful unions in the district. I pledged to serve a limited period of time, not to accept any special-interest money, not to accept honorariums, and try to be a more honest kind of congressman. Ironically, but consistently, I made the same pledges in my 2014 Senate campaign. These pledges forty years later included refusing to take special- interest money, focusing only on the issues facing South Dakotans, and pledging to serve only one Senate term. In 1974 and in 2014, I was driven by a desire to serve God and my fellow man—not donors.

Although I was born and bred in South Dakota, Republican leaders saw me as an interloper. In the far-flung precincts of South Dakota, my credentials as a Rhodes Scholar, Harvard Law School graduate, and Foreign Service Officer made me look like an elitist outsider.

Yet I made a strong impression on the voters during a primary debate. I declared that if I were a member of the House of Representatives, I would vote to give Richard Nixon a trial in the Senate. "It is the only way to get at the truth about Watergate," I said. This was a bit awkward, because many people knew I was a personal friend of Nixon's daughter. I emphasized that I liked President Nixon personally, but I was afraid that he had gotten into a situation that could only be resolved by a trial in the Senate.

When the votes in the Republican primary were counted, I managed to win the whirlwind three-way race by a narrow margin.

God clearly had plans for me. As I approached the general election, I started to wonder if I had bitten off more than I could chew. "I don't have any organization and I don't have any plan. I don't have any money," I complained to Dr. William Farber, my old political science professor and mentor at the University of South Dakota. "Well," Doc Farber replied, "did you have any of these things in the primary?" I didn't.

My father thought I was in over my head and that I was setting myself up for a big disappointment. My mother volunteered to help out. During the campaign, she wrote thank-you letters to people who contributed money. She answered my phone calls. Gradually, this quiet, shy farm woman, who hadn't graduated from high school, came out of her shell and began to enjoy the whirl of political life. Sadly, she wasn't able to participate in my 2014 campaign, as she passed away at the age of ninety-one in 2010.

The campaign was not without its humorous moments. At one point, people complained they had received thank- you letters from Mother in someone else's handwriting. I immediately "investigated" my mother, and discovered that she had fallen so far behind in her letter writing that she had indeed asked neighboring women to help her out by signing her letters. I 'fessed' up to this mini-scandal and it quickly went away. But most of the time, I was running scared. This campaign was a fearless and bold move, but the decision was just a continuation of a trend throughout my life: *I have always opted for public service.* And like previous bold moves in my life, it paid off. My bootstrap campaign and unorthodox methods of reaching out to voters turned out to be the perfect formula for electoral success.

In the end, I scored a stunning upset victory and won the election by 14,927 votes. I was one of very few Republicans in America who unseated an incumbent Democrat in the House that year—following President Gerald Ford's September pardon of former President Nixon. On the last day of the campaign, before the vote, I spent the balance of my modest funds on the following ad in the South Dakota newspapers.

Coincidentally, I used this same message in a "Thank You" television ad I produced the day before the 2014 election: "THANKS. I want to thank you, the people of South Dakota, for responding so well to my grassroots campaign. Together, we have done something unique in our time. We have successfully run a congressional campaign without any special-interest money. We have emphasized the good in our system. We have not been negative. More important, we have proved that politics can be positive, fun, issue-oriented, and close to the people."

CHAPTER 7

A "Hayseed from South Dakota" Comes to Washington

On January 3, 1975, when the day finally arrived for me to take my seat in the U.S. House of Representatives, I put on my best suit—a loud, plaid, off-the-rack number that plainly marked me as someone from the sticks—and entered the ornate House chamber. My parents, my sisters Beverly and Sandra, my brother Dan, my brother-in-law Roger, and my Aunt Annie watched from the packed Visitors' Gallery as I was sworn in. It was emotional for them and for me.

Despite the wise advice I received from many political "gray beards," I managed to make some serious mistakes during my first forays in Congress. During the election campaign, *Time* magazine had referred to me as a "McGovern Republican," because I was against the Vietnam War—even though I was a combat veteran. They were comparing me to the liberal Democrat and senior senator from my state, George McGovern. For my part, I defined myself as an independent, and was proud of it. I was used to speaking my mind. I was also one of very few Republicans to defeat an incumbent Democrat that year, so I had a bit of hubris entering office.

I was warned to be guarded and not reveal my true political feelings about the Vietnam War. The ornery Midwesterner in me believed that I could operate with impunity as an independent within my party's caucus. I soon learned otherwise. Whatever disagreements I had with my sweet-natured father didn't prepare me for dealing with 434 other members of the House of Representatives—hardened politicians who were driven by power and ambition and who gave no quarter. If I was going to carve out a successful career in Congress, I knew I had to adapt. I was no longer in 4-H—I was in Congress!

In the wake of my surprising 1974 election victory against an entrenched incumbent, I was eager to settle down to business in Congress. But that proved harder than I expected. Everyone was distracted by the national upheaval that was taking place at the other end of Pennsylvania Avenue in the White House.

Vice President Ford had recently replaced President Richard Nixon in the Oval Office. By January of 1975, the war in Vietnam was reaching its deathly climax. Though I was now an opponent of the Vietnam War, I couldn't help but feel sorry for my own party's man in the White House. Gerry Ford naturally wanted to avoid becoming the first president to preside over the defeat of the United States in a foreign war.

By the end of April, the die was cast: Communist forces were at the gates of Saigon, and Ford gave the order for Operation Frequent Wind—a helicopter evacuation from the roof of the United States Embassy. I was upset by the heartrending photos of the American flag being taken down from the embassy. The awful consequences of America's folly in Vietnam hit me personally like a ton of bricks, and I questioned even more the value of the two years I had spent in the military.

Nothing like this had happened before, and Washington was caught up in a frenzy of guilt and recrimination. In an effort to move on, President Ford declared, "The war in Vietnam is receding into history." However, as a Vietnam combat veteran, I knew that Ford was indulging in wishful thinking. The war overseas might be over, but the havoc it had wrought in our nation would not go away for a long, long time, nor would it stop torturing me personally. I was then and still am permanently wounded by that war, as is my whole generation.

But at the time, I had to focus on my new job. And I had a steep learning curve. Servicing constituents is tough, tedious, and grinding work. To help me handle the load, I had three service offices in South Dakota, in addition to my Washington operation. Typically, I'd fly home to South Dakota on Thursday night and attend a weekend full of parades (riding my John Deere tractor), "listening meetings" with constituents, and Sunday church services at which I'd frequently be asked to speak. In between, I did TV and radio infomercials urging people to get in touch with me about their problems (Social Security, farm subsidies, visa problems, small business loans, service academy nominations, and so on). I found the job of helping people satisfying. Day in and day out, I focused on the casework, which not only helped my constituents, but also helped me understand the need and demand for certain policy changes and legislation. I was reminded on a daily basis why I had been sent to Washington.

A lot of people in the media today like to talk about the good old days when courtesy, conviviality, and bipartisanship reigned in the House. But speak to anyone who was actually there in the 1970s, and they'll tell you that those memories are a figment of the imagination. Congress then was nowhere near as partisan as Congress is today, but the Democrats ruled the roost in the 1970s. The Republicans were just as partisan—they simply didn't have the power. I was a soft-edged, gentle guy from a rural state that was very far away from Washington, both geographically and culturally. I was a bit of a fish out of water—an outlier, independent even then.

Nonetheless, I managed to rack up some successes and learned how to become an effective legislator. Among other things, I sponsored successful amendments to Meals on Wheels for elderly shut-ins, and the Older Americans Act— which included matching funds for congregate housing. This idea allowed the elderly to live in individual apartments with common dining areas. It maintained a degree of independence for the elderly, and cost the government significantly less than full-time nursing care. I successfully negotiated three federally funded, major water pipelines through my state: the WEB Water pipeline, the Oglala pipeline, and the Lewis and Clark pipeline. Adequate drinking water has always been a serious problem in my state, especially on the Indian reservations, so these pipelines were very important. But they were also controversial, because many landowners didn't want a pipeline running through their property. I also sponsored the Vocational Education Act, and the establishment of junior colleges for Native Americans on reservations throughout the country.

The dedicated and tireless casework required to bring these projects to completion led to public opinion polls indicating that I was the most popular politician in South Dakota. I started receiving calls from around the state, encouraging me to run for Senate. I stepped up the pace of my listening meetings. During the August recess of 1977, I held sixty of them—not only in my congressional district, but also in the western part of the state. I was laying the groundwork for a statewide campaign.

In early 1978, I held a press conference at my family farm in Humboldt. My mother was in charge of greeting everyone, and my father—who was drifting into Alzheimer's—sat there in his overalls and listened to me announce my candidacy for the Senate. I wondered what he thought.

Once again manna rained down from heaven: 1978 turned out to be a Republican year, and I won the race with 68 percent of the vote, a state record for a Senate race. In January 1979, my friend Democratic Senator George McGovern escorted me down the aisle to the well of the Senate, where I was sworn in as the twenty-second senator from South Dakota since it had achieved statehood. I was a thirty-six-year-old Republican with a fiercely independent temperament and the first Vietnam veteran to be elected to the Senate.

CHAPTER 8

Reagan, Alzheimer's, and Me

In 1979, I met Ronald Reagan for the first time. I was on the presidential campaign plane with him, his wife, Nancy, and one of his top advisers, Martin Anderson. We were flying from Idaho to Rapid City, South Dakota, for a campaign event. On that flight, Governor Reagan was extremely nice to me and we talked about his Irish ancestry. I commented that I had one grandmother from Mayo County, Ireland, but that most of the rest of my ancestors were Danish. He asked me about the farm where I had grown up and we compared notes about small-town childhoods. I'm not sure what prompted me to share such a personal story with a perfect stranger, but I told him that I was worried about my dad. Although he had been a steady farmer for many decades, he was now acting strangely. He would take long walks by himself and just disappear into the cornfields.

At their peak, corn stalks can grow to about eight to ten feet high, so in a huge field, people can really get lost. Sometimes neighbors have to assemble search parties to find children who wander off into the cornfields. We had to do that several times for my dad. We would find him taking a nap. At the time, I didn't know what to make of it. I was so busy being a new congressman that I honestly compartmentalized it. I'm still not sure why I brought it up with Reagan.

That day, Reagan listened intently and sympathetically. Then the discussion quickly migrated to the irony of our supporting leftist regimes in Central America that were actually dictatorial. All this was, and still is, very controversial, as some of those wars and tensions are ongoing.

Fast-forward almost three years later to July of 1982. My dad's behavior had become more unpredictable and irrational. He was diagnosed with Alzheimer's disease. My mother insisted on caring for him at home, but we eventually had to place him in a nursing home. That summer, *People* magazine published an article about me and my dad and his heartbreaking decline into the fog of Alzheimer's. As I said in the article:

> I don't know how this thing could have been prevented, even if it had been diagnosed earlier. If it's Alzheimer's disease, as doctors now believe, there's no cure for it, and there probably wouldn't have been any difference in the sequence of events. It certainly points up the limits of our power as well as the fragility, the unpredictability of human existence. It seems very unfair to me, though, to see Dad in this condition. He would have been horrified because he never wanted to be dependent on anybody, and now he's spent the last few years totally dependent on other people. I've often imagined what he'd be like at this point if he were still healthy. He probably would have just kept on farming as his own father did, rather than taking Social Security. He enjoyed moving around and working the farm, and I'm sure he would still be going full speed if he only could.

The next week, I was sitting in a routine Senate Commerce Committee hearing when a young intern came up to me, wide-eyed, and said, "President Reagan wants to speak with you on the phone in the side office." I thought this was a prank, as there were lots of Ronald Reagan imitators around in those days, but I picked up the phone anyway and said, "Senator Pressler speaking."

On the other end of the line was an unmistakable, husky voice who replied, "This is Ron. I just read this article in People magazine and I cried a little bit. Why don't you come over and we'll talk about this?" I did, and we had a nice talk.

President Ronald Reagan and I became personal friends over our discussions of my father's Alzheimer's disease. Photo courtesy of the White House.

Later that year, he startled me by asking how my father was doing; his thoughtfulness to remember and inquire was surprising and touching. This concern of his became steadfast. In fact, Reagan asked me about my dad every few months. He also invited me to an Oval Office meeting on Alzheimer's—Princess Yasmin Khan, whose mother, the movie star Rita Hayworth, died from Alzheimer's, was being honored for her work on this issue. Alzheimer's research was underfunded then, as it is now.

In fact, even as the Baby Boom generation continues to age, we have failed to devote the money necessary to finding an effective treatment and cure for this dreaded disease. The princess has done remarkable work raising money for research, and has helped the public to overcome the stigma attached to the illness.

Several years later, when President Reagan issued his heartbreaking letter to the nation announcing his own diagnosis with the disease, I was dumbfounded and deeply saddened. He said he was withdrawing from public activities and entering "the sunset of my life." I saw him one more time at the Los Angeles Country Club a few years later and he was lucid—clear as a bell. I thought his withdrawal from public life was premature. I joked, "I bet you wrote that letter so you don't have to come to all those political things anymore." He chuckled and said, "Don't I wish."

I live in fear of an Alzheimer's diagnosis. I am constantly inspired, however, by Reagan's example. As he said in his letter, "In closing, let me thank you, the American people, for giving me the great honor of allowing me to serve as your president. When the Lord calls me home, whenever that may be, I will leave the greatest love for this country of ours and eternal optimism for its future." My sentiments exactly.

CHAPTER 9

Glory and Compromise in Three Senate Terms

As senators, George McGovern and I represented very different faces of South Dakota. He was a decorated World War II combat aviator, a B-24 pilot who had risen to national prominence as the leader of his party's anti–Vietnam War wing—in contrast, I was a Vietnam veteran who had become disenchanted with our country's military adventures. George was a hero of the Democratic Party's far left wing; he had lost the 1972 presidential election to my friend Richard Nixon in the second-biggest landslide in American history. I was a moderate conservative who had won a seat in the Senate without the wholehearted support of the hard-core conservatives who increasingly controlled the Republican Party. Despite our political differences, George and I genuinely liked each other.

As the only Vietnam combat veteran in the U.S. Senate at the time, I questioned the size and influence of what President Dwight Eisenhower had termed the U.S. military- industrial complex. I also doubted the wisdom of spending hundreds of billions of dollars to keep huge phalanxes of our fighting forces overseas. My stand on these issues put me in a good light with some Midwestern Republican conservatives, who generally opposed using ground forces abroad. On fiscal matters, I voted conservative. I was never very active on the social issues; I was more of an economic Republican, interested in economic growth, stimulating investment and new jobs through wise taxation policies.

However, I didn't hesitate to vote against the conservatives when I felt strongly about an issue. I cosponsored the Equal Rights Amendment for women, and I voted with moderates and liberals on arms control. Wyoming Senator Alan Simpson called me "predictably unpredictable."

Just when President Ronald Reagan was entering the White House, I became chairman of the Arms Control Subcommittee of the Senate Foreign Relations Committee. Riding Reagan's coattails in 1980, the Republicans gained control of the Senate for the first time since the 1950s.

Critics charged that Reagan was a passive, incurious president who glossed over details, even suggesting that he had Alzheimer's while he was in office. I never saw any evidence of this. On the contrary, Reagan knew the arcane details of arms control like nobody else in Washington. He and I saw eye-to-eye on this issue from the very start of my chairmanship and his presidency. Indeed, arms control was high on Reagan's personal agenda, and he made it a point to invite me to the Oval Office for cabinet-level meetings on a number of occasions. He always encouraged me to speak my mind. Many of the others at those meetings, including the Pentagon brass, assumed that a staunch conservative like Reagan couldn't possibly work with the Russians on reducing arms or limiting arms sales with developing countries. They were wrong.

Reagan was particularly interested in my views on the Indian subcontinent's balance of power, namely, that between India and Pakistan. He told me that he admired me for not reflexively supporting the concept of "mutually assured destruction," or "MAD" in the shorthand acronym. He opposed it as well, often remarking that it was called MAD "for a reason."

In those days, a virtual priesthood of arms control experts held long conclaves to study each new proposal for a U.S.-U.S.S.R. treaty, which usually allowed each side to build more nuclear weapons. The limitation defined in these treaties was to allow for an increase of weapons by each side—a limitation in increase but never a real reduction. I was considered a rogue newcomer in the arms control debate because I boldly said that the United States should seek to reduce or eliminate nuclear weapons worldwide. On one occasion, a group of cabinet-level officials—including Vice President George Bush—was sitting in the Oval Office, and the president went around the room asking everyone's opinion in turn. I was the only one to speak for the idea that we should start pursuing a total reduction or elimination of nuclear weapons worldwide. In the end Reagan asked, "I've only heard one opinion on reducing nuclear weapons. Everyone else wants limited increases. Why on earth don't we accept Senator Pressler's view?"

Defense Secretary Caspar Weinberger, the leading hawk present, responded, "Because Senator Pressler does not know arms control very well." It was a nasty put-down and meant to embarrass me as the conversation moved on to arcane, alphabet-soup territory.

Reagan seemed to like my plain speaking—or "plains speaking," as we say on the prairie. In any case, the moment came when he said, "I want you to keep meeting with my foreign policy team." At that, National Security Advisor William Clark visibly cringed and gritted his teeth.

How did I get included in meetings with Reagan? As chairman of the subcommittee, I was naturally invited to many of them. But when the Pentagon brass saw that I was able to pass amendments and actually began to influence Reagan, they complained to Reagan's presidential assistant, Michael Deaver, and asked him to limit my access. Luckily, Deaver liked me and even agreed with me. He coached me, telling me that a way to see the president personally without getting on his official schedule was to attend the signing ceremonies for bills that crossed his desk. After these short ceremonies, Deaver would arrange for me to walk back to the Oval Office with Reagan. He and I would have a conversation that would not show up on the president's schedule, and the Pentagon generals and admirals and bureaucrats would not be alerted every time I spoke with their boss. Access to the president is one of the hardest things to get in Washington. Petty little wars of jealousy can fester quickly over which officials get more.

I met several times with President Ronald Reagan in the Oval Office with his Cabinet foreign policy team, including this meeting in September 1982. Pictured left to right: Secretary of State James Baker, President Reagan, Vice President George Bush, Senator Larry Pressler, Deputy Secretary of State Ken Dam, and National Security Advisor William Clark. Photo courtesy of the White House.

With President Reagan's encouragement, I worked on an amendment to the Foreign Assistance Act of 1961. Called the

"Pressler Amendment," this piece of legislation banned economic and military assistance to Pakistan unless the president could certify that Pakistan didn't possess a nuclear device. It also placed a trade embargo on Pakistan and blocked the delivery of certain fighter jets and military equipment there if the president could not make the nonnuclear certification.

President George H. W. Bush enforced the "Pressler Amendment" from the day he came into office. His policy initiative worked. Pakistan backed down on its nuclear program during the four years that Bush "41" was in office, 1989 to 1993. When he enforced the amendment, he ran into opposition from what I have come to call the "Octopus," but still he imposed the sanctions and made them stick— pursuing a policy that may even have contributed to his defeat when he sought a second term in office.

The "Octopus" is the great-great-grandchild of the military-industrial complex, the pestiferous creature President Eisenhower named in his farewell address to the American people in 1961. That relatively simple organism mutated and evolved over three decades into a true monster as it enlisted other players into its circle, namely, leading academic institutions, research scientists, the major media, and cutting-edge technology. I call this MIASM-O—for Military-Industrial-Academic-Scientific-Media-Octopus—the "Octopus" for short.

The "Pressler Amendment" was one of those rare instances since World War II where Congress took a leading role in foreign policy. It is usually the president who sets the foreign policy agenda, as occurred with the Marshall Plan, the Korean War, and the Vietnam War; Congress then appropriated the monies for the funding. In other words, Congress traditionally plays a supporting role. The "Pressler Amendment" turned that tradition on its head. It also made me a household name in India and Pakistan and in foreign policy circles around the world. Its impact was much greater than many laws and presidential declarations. It became the lynchpin of the annual foreign policy debates on the floor of Congress for nearly a decade. The Pentagon strongly opposed it at the time, and the Octopus didn't really like it, either. But most defense and foreign policy experts today laud the "Pressler Amendment" and its effects. The policy became the cornerstone of our nuclear nonproliferation efforts.

In 1995, I became chairman of the Senate Commerce Committee. I was delighted with the assignment because one of the bills I was most interested in was a rewrite of the Communications Act of 1934. Since 1992, I had worked unsuccessfully on a rewrite of the act. Two bills that had passed in the Senate had died in the House. Now I had a chance to take a leadership role, and I went to work. I visited every single member of the Senate and more than 150 members of the House. After I found out what each one of them wanted in the bill and negotiated the bill's language with them, we worked out a bipartisan bill that passed—at the end of a very tough three-year fight. The Telecommunications Act of 1996 was a huge bill, the *magnum opus* of my time in the Senate, and one for which I am known nationally in the United States. Like every major piece of legislation that has become law, it was many years in the making. By the 1970s, it was clear that the Communications Act of 1934 was obsolete. If the United States was to be a world leader in telecommunications—as it must be—that old patchwork of laws had to be replaced. The new law had to be cogent, effective, and comprehensive. At the same time, it had to cover a multitude of particulars. It had to recognize the complexities of modern telecommunications, recognize the realities of an international environment, acknowledge marketplace forces, encourage research and development, and benefit the American people in the long run. This was clear to everyone in the telecommunications industry, to members of the relevant committees in Congress, and to everyone with any kind of stake in electronic communications.

As a member of the Senate Commerce Committee, I decided to take up this cause, and to make it my cause, in part because the people of South Dakota could only keep up with the rest of the world if they were "connected"—and in the years to come that meant linked via the new electronic media.

In the bill, we created a nongovernmental fund that diverts a tiny fraction of a cent of every dollar collected by telecommunications companies to a "universal service fund." This fund provides a subsidy to inner-city and rural telecommunications providers. As a result, rural South Dakota benefited enormously, but this was not apparent in 1996 when the bill first passed. Today, when I walk around and I see the large number of cell phones and computers being used, I feel a great sense of satisfaction.

The cost of a telephone call per minute is less than it was when I was a young person. Texting and emailing cost less now than in the 1990s. The word "long distance call" has been dropped from our vocabulary. For the first time, all the companies in the telecommunications industry worked together. We couldn't have the Internet as we know it today without the Telecommunications Act of 1996! Vice President Gore took a lot of the credit for this law when he intemperately claimed to have helped "invent the Internet." He and President Clinton presided over the signing ceremony, but I knew who had done the lion's share of the detailed legislative work in the trenches to get it passed.

Despite all this good work on behalf of the constituents in my state, I lost my reelection bid for the Senate in 1996. When anyone loses a political race, he or she usually blames someone else or certain circumstances. I principally blame myself. Maybe, after twenty-two years in Congress, I was burned out. I had spent all of my evenings and most Saturdays in 1995 working around the clock on that massive bill. For the first time in my life and just a year away from reelection, I was not doing my listening meetings with the same regularity in my state. Working on the telecommunications bill seemed subconsciously to transcend everything else. As the new chairman of the Senate Commerce Committee, I had wanted to pass a major bill that would give Americans widespread access to the Internet.

All excuses aside, part of the reason I might have lost is a tradition in South Dakota we call "Karl's Curse." Many politicians don't survive after three terms. George McGovern didn't, Tom Daschle didn't (and he was the Senate majority leader!), and I didn't. The only South Dakota politician to be elected to a fourth term was Karl Mundt—and he suffered a stroke during his fourth term. The message from South Dakota voters is clear: they like term limits, and three terms seems to be their limit.

After twenty-two years in elected office, I was now out of a job. I wrote a humorous editorial in *The New York Times* in 1997, talking about how I was learning to use a fax machine. I practiced law for a few years and served as a corporate director on a variety of boards in India, England, Vietnam, and the United States. But teaching has occupied most of my time and it is one of my life's passions. I have taught at a variety of schools all over the world: Harvard University, Baruch College (teaching and serving on the board of directors of the School of Public Administration); the Indian National University in Bangalore, West Point, the University of Paris (Sciences Po), Bar-Alan University in Tel Aviv, the University of Bologna in Italy as a Fulbright professor, the University of California in Los Angeles as a senior fellow, the University of Sioux Falls, the University of South Dakota, six Chinese universities, and two Native-American colleges. Teaching is not financially lucrative, but it is satisfying and it has fulfilled my need to serve the public. I fully intended to ride into the sunset with my career in Congress complete.

And so I surprised even myself when, almost two decades later, I decided to run for public office again.

I served on the board of directors for seven years at Infosys, an Indian company. In 2013 I participated in the opening ceremony as honorary chairman when the company became listed on the New York Stock Exchange. Photo courtesy of the New York Stock Exchange.

CHAPTER 10

Diving Back In: Running an Idealistic Campaign

W hile staying busy in my home state and elsewhere after losing my 1996 reelection bid for the Senate, I watched in dismay from the sidelines as politics in Washington became increasingly dysfunctional. The insane partisan fighting was dragging our nation down.

I am still the moderate centrist that I was in Congress, but the GOP has moved far to the right—now neither party works well with the other. Both the Republicans and Democrats are locked into a "lobbyist-controlled- spending-and-taxing" cycle. And they are both mired in poisonous partisan fights where nothing is resolved. I wanted to break that stranglehold.

The open Senate seat in 2014 in South Dakota presented a rare opportunity for an Independent. I also knew that I could have a very good chance of winning the Republican primary, and may have won, but then I would be committed to joining a traditional caucus. That was not at all appealing to me. If elected, I wanted to be truly independent in Congress, able to vote with either caucus and not obligated to either party or any interest group. I wanted to be able to work with both sides. Indeed, a core group of Independents in Congress could be part of the solution—the group of politicians that finally ends that bickering.

Currently one of the most influential men in the U.S. Senate is Senator Angus King of Maine, an Independent and a fiscal moderate who has been able to work with both parties. He was my model. South Dakota needed a powerful Independent U.S. senator to speak for its citizens on state and national matters. Recent statistics show that almost 90,000 South Dakotans are now registered Independents (out of 300,000 voters). We have many problems in Washington; as an Independent, I knew I could work with both sides and the president to gain fair treatment for South Dakota. The prospect of being freed from the political party strings was a dream.

To "test the waters" on a potential Independent candidacy, I began reaching out to some colleagues and former advisers to get their feedback—and a reality check. In late 2013, I had dinner with my longtime friend, Don Frankenfeld, in Rapid City. Don and I have known each other since the 1970s, when he was serving in the South Dakota State Legislature and I was a freshman congressman. Over the course of a leisurely dinner with his family, we discussed the possibility of my running for the U.S. Senate as an Independent.

As Don later said, "I was kind of shocked at the audacity of it. After taking a minute or two to digest his question, I felt really exhilarated because I think the idea of a third way is appealing to me." Frankenfeld is not a fan of either of the major parties and he told me he thought I was uniquely situated to overcome the natural disadvantages that most Independent candidates face—a lack of name recognition. On the contrary, I was already a familiar face to South Dakotans. Plus, I had a legitimate track record as a moderate.

But Don and I were also both realistic. Running a campaign for Senate as an Independent was going to be costly and my chances of winning were small. Don agreed, but said something to me in a subsequent conversation that I will always remember: "The journey is more important than the destination." He thought the campaign could benefit from a higher level of conversation *if I were in it*. As he saw it, my running in 2014 would be "a noble, patriotic sacrifice, but a quixotic effort that might—if everything fell together in just the right way—lead to success."

Another longtime South Dakota politico named Ted Thoms also encouraged me to run. He had recently left the Democratic Party and registered as an Independent because he was totally disgusted with both of the major parties who, he says, have "sold their soul to Wall Street." We didn't know each other well before the 2014 campaign, but he had read one of the monthly editorials I had penned in a South Dakota newspaper where I asserted that our country is spending too much money on overseas wars. It struck a chord with him.

He sent me a note and said he totally agreed with everything in my column. He urged me to run for the Senate as an Independent, contrary to much of the advice I was getting from others. I invited him to have lunch with me and we struck up a friendship. It was that day that Ted convinced me. My feelings about staging another Senate campaign— this time as an Independent—just clicked. He offered to set up ten meetings with his business friends across South Dakota to help me get started. He also offered to help with fundraising, and I accepted.

From these conversations, I slowly developed the idea to run an experimental, idealistic campaign. I was determined to run a low-budget campaign with only positive ads or positive messaging, and with no response to negative ads and messaging. In debates and forums, I would flat-out address the issues and pretty much ignore any personal matters. Pledging to serve only one six-year term, I vowed not to raise any money once elected because I would not want to get back into the big fundraising efforts that U.S. senators have to make. Since senators spend up to half their time raising money, it really distracts them from the business of legislating. I would only go back into the Senate if I could have six years without having to raise a dime for the next term.

My platform was idealistic in that I would try to become a truly independent *and* Independent U.S. senator. I might caucus with one side or the other, for a time. My dream was that there might be three to five Independent senators elected in 2014. U.S. Senate rules, unlike most state legislative rules, do provide for Independents to either remain Independent, or to join a caucus, or to switch caucuses. They have tremendous flexibility. There have been eight Independent senators during my lifetime. Former Senator Joe Lieberman of Connecticut said that his power in the Senate actually increased when he became an Independent because he could work with both sides more comfortably.

I had a vision to be a part of changing American politics. It can still be done. As the nonprofit organization, The Centrist Project, suggests, if we could elect up to five Independent U.S. senators, the whole landscape of American politics would change by breaking the poisonous deadlock between Republicans and Democrats. The Centrist Project has made its goal to elect five Independent senators in 2016 and 2018.

My campaign of 2014 had two goals: (1) I would run an idealistic campaign to set an example, and (2) if elected, I would serve as an Independent U.S. senator and help change the politics and history of the United States. It remains my conviction that this is a true solution to our current national crisis.

As I began to share my unofficial intentions with more and more people, word started to spread around political circles that I was considering a candidacy. Local and political media also heard the rumors and they had their own reactions. Most of them wrote off my campaign as too unlikely, but they *all* were intrigued with my boldness. In November of 2013, the *National Journal* wrote, "Pressler is right: He's a long shot. But his authenticity and candid comments could spice up an otherwise boring race. With polls reporting record dissatisfaction with the federal government, his candidacy could test whether voters would ever actually turn to an independent candidacy as an outlet for their frustration."

And then I caught a break when *American Hustle* was released in mid-December. There was immediately a lot of publicity and Oscar buzz surrounding this film, and that created new interest in the ABSCAM scandal—more than thirty years later. All of a sudden, national media were calling me to talk about my involvement in ABSCAM and how I was the only elected official to turn down the bribe. The timing of the movie's release was unrelated and coincidental to my planned Senate campaign announcement, but the film helped reintroduce me to a national audience.

I knew the GOP would consider me a "spoiler." I was not at all deterred. I was seventy-one years old, still healthy, and still eager to contribute to my nation. After all, throughout my life, I have always opted for public service. Idealism and my faith in God have always driven my commitment to my career and my activities. This decision was just one more example.

Accordingly, between Christmas and New Year's Eve in 2013, I held a series of press conferences across the state— Sioux Falls, Watertown, Aberdeen, and Rapid City—to formally announce my Independent candidacy for the U.S. Senate. I dove back into the fray.

CHAPTER 11

Game Changer– Native Americans and Mormonism

"Pressler could be a game-changer!" That's what one of the leading newspapers in South Dakota, The *Watertown Public Opinion*, called my candidacy in a thoughtful editorial published on New Year's Eve day in 2013: "Although somewhat of a long shot, it's not out of the question... [I]f Pressler can pull enough votes away from whomever the GOP and Democratic nominees are, coupled with those who traditionally avoid voting for major party candidates, he could find himself back on Capitol Hill."

The paper also laid out the national stakes for the 2014 elections very clearly: "Republicans need a net gain of six seats to capture control of the Senate from Democrats, who effectively hold a 55–45 advantage now. Democrats will be defending 21 of 35 seats to be decided in November... that's where independents like [Angus] King... and perhaps the potentially newly elected Pressler could come into play. They could hold the keys to deciding things one way or another in the Senate."

The article applauded my pledge not to engage in any fundraising and to serve just one term, making it clear that my focus would be on South Dakota's interests and not my next election.

Of course, this news piece made me even more excited and

determined about my decision to run. But now I had to get down to "brass tacks" and get enough petition signatures that were required for an Independent to get on the ballot in South Dakota. By state law, I couldn't begin to collect those signatures until January 1, 2014, and I had an April deadline to submit and certify the petitions. Independents didn't have to go through the primary process, but we did have to solicit more signatures than the Republicans or Democrats are required to collect. It was a big chore, and took sixty to seventy volunteers to complete the task. They hiked all over the state to get the job done, going door to door and standing outside of grocery stores, churches, and public events. The experience reminded me of collecting signatures for my first campaign in 1974, when I also had no party apparatus behind me to guide and assist me. Ironically, I was back where I started. This time, of course, I had name recognition and a track record to boost my efforts.

It was during this time that I first noticed a disturbing trend among the youth of our country—near total apathy for politics. I spent one morning in Brookings at the South Dakota State University student union. I set up a table to collect petition signatures from registered voters. I couldn't believe how few students were registered. Although I was well received by the students, there was just a flat response on politics. Many of them would be chatting very enthusiastically with me, but when I asked them if they were registered to vote, they would give me a rather bewildered look. Contrast that with my visit later that afternoon to the Brookings Senior Center. Not surprisingly, they recognized me from my time in elected office. But, more important, they were *all* registered to vote and they offered to take more petitions to circulate. Despite their age, they were engaged in the political process.

One of the most important constituencies in South Dakota was the Native American community. I had a long history of working with them, so I was determined to spend significant time on the reservations during this campaign. They represent approximately 8.9 percent, or 74,000, of the total population of South Dakota (according to 2012 population figures from the Census Bureau). They were and are my friends. I had worked tirelessly on their behalf during my time in elected office, meeting with each of the tribes at least annually and visiting every reservation. The tribal leaders' input on legislation that would affect their people was important to me because it was important to them.

When I served in the Senate, at least two of my staff were devoted full time to Native American issues and legislation. Constantly seeking ways to increase their sovereignty and to defend their rights, I was the main sponsor of the legislation creating Tribally Controlled Colleges throughout the United States, including South Dakota. When the Oglala Sioux Tribe was trying to bring a lawsuit against the U.S. government in the late 1970s, I helped them navigate a roadblock that would have prevented them from suing. Their ensuing litigation resulted in the Black Hills Claims Settlement. In fact, the Supreme Court quoted my speech given on the House floor in *United States v. Sioux Nation of Indians*. The Supreme Court rarely quotes a member of Congress, so this legislative accomplishment ranks near the top of my lifetime achievements. It was a fairly high political risk, but I thought it was the right thing to do. Native American rights are fundamental civil rights.

One of the first influential people to come forward to help me in 2014 was Tim Giago, a Harvard-educated Native American who had been born and raised on a reservation in South Dakota. He is a publisher of several successful newspapers and a national leader in the Native American community. Frustrated by the lack of progress that elected officials in South Dakota were making to improve the Native American condition, he had become an

Independent and, in several newspaper editorials in 2012 and 2013, encouraged more Native Americans to follow his lead and register as Independents. That way, he said, neither party could take their vote for granted.

It was "Publisher Giago," as he is affectionately known, who ran the front-page story and photo back in November of 2013 in the *Native Sun News* that headlined my exploring a run for the Senate. It was the first major statewide and nationwide publicity for me—even if I hadn't yet made it official.

Embarking on a type of tribal "listening tour" of the reservations in our state early in 2014, I got on the road to collect petition signatures and remind the tribes of my legislative history defending and advocating for them. The problems of the nine Native American tribal governments in South Dakota have long perplexed me. I came to believe that all my work in getting more federal payments for the Indians while I was serving in Congress was not really solving the root of their problems. Statistics have shown that up to 75 percent of Native Americans on the Pine Ridge Reservation suffer from alcoholism. Twenty-five percent suffer from the effects of fetal alcohol syndrome. Several church groups were doing some pretty innovative charity work with the Native Americans, most notably the Church of Jesus Christ of Latter-day Saints. I began to believe that their lifestyle—one of prayer, work, sobriety, and generosity—might be part of the solution. I do not think one church or belief is better than any other—and I will not argue the doctrinal differences of churches—but the Mormons' anonymous acts of charity in their local communities inspired me. I wanted to emulate them.

In the 2014 campaign, I observed closely and personally the active life of charity that some Mormons lived with our native peoples. On one hot August day of urban campaigning, I watched a Mormon woman in Sioux Falls give her "fast offering" to an inner-city Native American single mother of three. She took her to a food store to buy fruits and vegetables, much more expensive than the young mother could afford, and much more healthful than her children's usual diet. Then the kind Mormon woman took her charitable gesture the extra mile. She taught the impoverished Indian woman how to prepare nutritious meals for her children—because in central Sioux Falls they had been subsisting only on junk food. Her selfless act, her "work is prayer," will have effects far more consequential than if she had simply given the Indian woman cash.

In South Dakota the generosity some Mormons show for the Native American people has impressed me. Over the last forty-five years, a series of coincidences in my life had led me to consider joining the Mormon faith. I have befriended many Mormons who were "ordinary people." In addition, I have met some famous ones: about a dozen senators and congressmen, my former campaign pollster Richard Wirthlin, Republican Senator Orrin Hatch, Republican Senator Paula Hawkins, Harvard Business School professor Clayton Christensen—and, in particular, Democratic Senator Harry Reid (Senator Reid really made my conversion happen for me!). Charity, of course, is only a stopgap in easing the plight of Native Americans. They have to become more self-sufficient. Therefore, I wanted to promote and endorse ways their communities were helping themselves.

During the spring and summer of the 2014 campaign, I identified a series of promising new initiatives and projects being proposed and tested by the Native American community, and decided to make them a keystone of my campaign. If elected, I pledged to sponsor legislation and federal funding for some of these programs. One of those ideas was a Native American Holocaust Memorial Museum. Developed over several years by Publisher Giago, this proposal would locate the museum in Wounded Knee, in western South Dakota; I thought it could have satellite locations in other states where Indian massacres have occurred. Publisher Giago felt this museum could be a major tourist attraction, and I agreed with him. He believed strongly that the term "holocaust" was appropriate, even though some Jewish people were protective of the term.

I learned of the intense interest internationally in the Native American condition as a Fulbright professor in Europe, a part-time assignment I have held for several years. When I would give a carefully prepared lecture on foreign policy, the European students would come up to me after class and say they had noticed I was from South Dakota.

Then they would request a lecture on the Native American Indians, not just the story of those from South Dakota but of all the North American tribes. The level of knowledge and interest in Native Americans that I observed when I lectured for the Fulbright program at universities in Germany and at the University of Paris was amazing. These students know much more about Native Americans than we Americans do. I was touched when some students gave me books on Red Cloud and other Native Americans as a farewell present.

Publisher Giago's idea was as big as Mount Rushmore. There is no Native American holocaust museum in existence, yet there are some seventy World War II–related holocaust museums around the world. The time has come for a major world-class holocaust museum at Wounded Knee, South Dakota. In 2014 I pledged that one of my first acts as a newly elected senator would be to sponsor legislation to secure federal funding to make this vision a reality.

On one visit to the Rosebud Indian Reservation in south central South Dakota for a meeting with the tribal president, I was impressed with an aquaculture development project he and the tribal leadership team showed me. They had spent two years building a greenhouse to grow and market tilapia fish. It was encouraging. Here was a project that could create real jobs that pay real wages and produce real products for profit, all done within the reservation. It promised to help Rosebud become more self-sufficient and could be a template for other reservations to implement—exactly the kind of project for Native Americans to help themselves that I wanted to work for again in the Senate.

Previously, I had been a sponsor of "Operation Bootstrap," a program that would help private development of businesses and jobs on the reservation. We need real business plans, real bank loans, and real cooperation with the federal government to develop jobs and economic development on the reservations. When I learned about the tilapia project, I pledged to make this a legislative priority, too.

During my 2014 Senate campaign, Gerald One Feather died. This legendary Oglala Sioux leader and former tribal president from the Pine Ridge Indian Reservation was one of my lifelong friends from our University of South Dakota days. Gerald was the founder of the community college in Oglala that served as the model for the legislation I sponsored to create Native American community colleges nationwide. Just before he died, he told his wife that he wanted to vote for me and he lightheartedly said to her that he wanted to make a "deathbed endorsement" of my Senate campaign.

My wife, Harriet, and I spent two days at Gerald's wake and funeral. The wake was held in a large tent on the grounds of a casino hotel on the reservation. When we walked in, we felt like we had walked into a Native American art gallery. The tent walls were covered—floor to ceiling—in "star quilts," and the space was surrounded by tables covered in colorful gifts to the family: artwork, jewelry, personal notes and tributes to Gerald, photos, antiques, and more quilts. The richness of the décor was overwhelming. A steady drum was beating. Gerald's open casket was in the center of the room. Attendees lined up to pay their final respects. Some placed private messages and pieces of jewelry in the casket. It was my special honor to place his war bonnet in his casket.

Mrs. One Feather (center) presented me a funeral tribal quilt just before I gave the eulogy at my friend Gerald One Feather's funeral on the Pine Ridge Indian Reservation. Also pictured is Harriet Pressler (left) and me. Photo courtesy of Oglala Sioux Tribe.

My eulogy was heartfelt: "Gerald One Feather's life will be an inspiration to me to sponsor legislation, if I am sent back to the Senate, to expand the tribal community colleges, particularly in the technology area, so that our Native Americans can be totally competitive in today's markets." We were seated in the second row for the service, just behind Gerald's immediate family. In the middle of the ceremony, I was stunned when Gerald's widow presented me a tribal star quilt and publicly recognized me for my work on behalf of the Native American people during my twenty-two years in Congress. It was an honor I didn't expect, but one I will always cherish. It reminded me why and for whom I was running.

CHAPTER 12

On the "Comeback Trail": A Majestic and Spiritual Experience

"Majestic" and "spiritual" are words used to describe the landscape in South Dakota, and at no time is that more evident than during the winter. On one of my first state driving tours early in the campaign, Harriet and I stopped in Kennebec, a small town in the middle of ranching territory in the state. It is also the home town and resting place of the late Senator Jim Abdnor. As colleagues in the U.S. House, Jim and I had our differences sometimes, but we were still friends. I hadn't really had a chance to say goodbye to him properly. We decided to pay a visit to his grave, which was located in a small cemetery on a large hill on the outskirts of town.

It had snowed that morning, so there was a fresh and undisturbed blanket covering the ground around us. The day was sunny and cold. The bitter air made you catch your breath while the sun was blinding to the naked eye. We got out of the car and hiked up to the top of the hill. Trudging upward and focusing on our steps, we didn't notice the view until we reached the top of the hill.

We stopped, looked around, and it was truly awe- inspiring. We were overwhelmed by the majestic beauty of South Dakota. We could probably see seventy or eighty miles in every direction—

no crops, just snow-covered pasture. I suddenly felt very small and was reminded that I am just one person on this vast and beautiful place called earth. It felt like God's great spirit was rushing right through me, through my DNA—my very essence as a South Dakotan, an American, a creature of God. I had a sudden validation that I was doing the right thing, as long as I just kept turning my will over to the power of a higher authority.

About this time, in early 2014, most of the significant reforms of the Affordable Care Act, President Obama's controversial health care reform, were taking effect. The law, often called Obamacare, was still being hotly debated in the media, even after the Supreme Court had upheld the constitutionality of Obamacare's individual mandate in June 2012. I watched as Republican after Republican appeared on television talk shows and said they were going to repeal it, while every Democrat reflexively and uncritically lauded its merits.

I was reminded of the fact that if Republican Governor Mitt Romney had been elected in 2012, we probably would have been debating an almost identical bill—something called "Romneycare." The fact is that when Romney was governor of Massachusetts, his state passed a similar health care reform law in 2006, with a similar individual mandate. Every Republican would have rallied behind "Romneycare," and every Democrat would have been against it. It is just one example of the irrational partisan gridlock that exists in this country. Nobody focuses on the policy itself. They just want to bicker about who's right and who's wrong.

Everyone seems to agree that our nation needs comprehensive health care reform. This law has some laudable goals. I argued that South Dakota's rural communities need health care cooperatives. I invited President Obama to my state to discuss how we can improve the law to help South Dakotans—especially those residents on Indian reservations. The law is not perfect, but what law is? If I were elected senator, I would work to improve the law, not repeal it. Obamacare provided just one more reason why I was running.

I rented a small office space in downtown Sioux Falls and hired a young college graduate, Colin O'Neal, to help me. He was my only paid campaign employee. My wife, Harriet, agreed to be my driver. (She says that I talk on the phone too much in the car to do both at the same time!) Because I entered the race late, I spent almost the entire first three months getting the statewide petition process completed.

Consequently, I played catch-up for most of the rest of 2014. With very little money and no political party machine to back me up, I was on my own. Luckily, some of the early supporters I garnered in the Native American community gave me a necessary initial, statewide publicity boost. This helped me collect the required petition signatures.

I was also fortunate to receive public support from some prominent Democrats *and* Republicans in my state. Lifelong Democrat and my former U.S. Senate campaign opponent Ted Muenster, president emeritus of the USD Foundation, circulated petitions for me. Former GOP state lawmaker Gene Abdallah publicly endorsed me. And, of course, I had my "kitchen cabinet" of Don Frankenfeld, Ted Thoms, Mike Kirby, Jerry Thirstrup, and many of my old 4-H buddies.

In March, the *Yankton County Observer* editorialized that my campaign was on the "comeback trail": "Forty years ago, a young fellow by the name of Larry Pressler moved back home to South Dakota and ran for U.S. Congress against Rep. Frank Denholm of Brookings. Denholm was judged unbeatable. He was an auctioneer, attorney, and FBI agent before entering politics, and he was instrumental in writing the 1974 Farm Bill. But when the votes were counted, South Dakota had a new congressman. Denholm was the only incumbent Democrat to lose in that

Watergate year of 1974... While it seems a monumental task for the state's '70s political wonder boy to make a comeback in 2014, it should be interesting to watch." Indeed.

All this complimentary media coverage was helpful in these first few months of the campaign, but it didn't help this Independent raise a lot of money. As I watched the Republican and Democratic candidates solicit and collect exponentially more than I was raising, the issue of campaign finance reform continued to weigh on me. Then on April 2, 2014, in the ruling on the case of *McCutcheon v. Federal Election Commission*, the Supreme Court struck down 1970s-era limits that individual donors can contribute to candidates and political committees. I disagreed with this decision.

First, I must admit that I do not have a simple solution to the outcome of this Supreme Court ruling, which followed the controversial *Citizens United* case in 2010. Over time, I had been conferring with a few people on a constitutional amendment that would allow limits to be set on campaign contributions and on lobbying expenditures. I met with the groups No Labels and The Centrist Project, both of which want to find ways to break the political logjam in Washington, but with different approaches. The Centrist Project subsequently endorsed me early in 2014—I was the new organization's first endorsed candidate.

What the Supreme Court ruling in *McCutcheon* did was to strengthen my resolve not to conduct *any* fundraising if I was elected. Zero. I wanted to be a senator who did not have to raise any money while in office. Everywhere I went in those early months of the campaign, I pounded home this message.

On a bitterly cold, wintry day in March, I rode in one of South Dakota's largest parades, the annual St. Patrick's Day parade in Sioux Falls. A railroad town, Sioux Falls originally attracted the Irish immigrants who built the railroads, so in addition to Scandinavians, the state is full of Irish Americans. This parade is popular—it attracted some 20,000 people in 2014, snow flurries and heavy winds notwithstanding (South Dakotans are rarely deterred by cold weather; they just bundle up). My friend Bob Christenson made the arrangements for me to ride in a 1949 Mercury convertible and recruited his teenage daughter and her friends to carry Pressler banners. Despite the cold, the girls had fun—it was their first campaign experience.

The crowds cheered me on when I passed them on the parade route. As many parades do, the procession was slow and the parade frequently stalled, so I would get out of the car to shake hands (and keep warm!). The reception was encouraging. It was the type of campaign event that I love to do, but this time I did not have the staff to follow behind me and collect names and contact information. It is important to do this to "harvest" the support you encounter along the campaign trail. You must take the warm reception and convert it to volunteer hours and high-volume, low-dollar financial contributions. We didn't have the staff or resources to do this. As a result, we "spilled a lot of milk." In other words, we couldn't take advantage of all the good will we were generating. It was a lost opportunity.

On April 14, 2014, I filed the required Federal Election Commission (FEC) report for the first quarter. It showed $36,749.19 cash on hand, up from a starting balance of $25,155.92. The report showed a loan from my personal bank account to the campaign of $29,873.61, and $9,580.00 received from individual contributors. Campaign expenses were $27,860.00 during this period. When I entered the race, I acknowledged that fundraising would be the most difficult part, because very few individuals, PACs, or groups ever give to Independent candidates. The principal reason is that an Independent will not be tied to the usual caucus setup, and contributors will have neither party leverage nor control over an Independent's votes. This circumstance would give South Dakota a truly independent voice in the Senate, but it also meant that fundraising would be extremely challenging. I was on track to set a record for the lowest-budget campaign in South Dakota Senate history.

It was a snowy day and I froze in an open convertible in South Dakota's largest St. Patrick's Day parade. Photo courtesy of Bob Christensen.

CHAPTER 13

Disrupting the Two-Party System

I had forgotten how exhausting the tempo of a campaign can be, but it sure felt good to be back in the game again. Every day, I awoke early and visited local coffee shops and diners to shake hands and talk with voters on their way to work. Many people in South Dakota are early risers and sharing coffee with them is a good way to get to know them in small groups in a casual setting. My goal was simple, but it required getting out every day and talking to voters, telling them why I was running and why they could expect something different from me if they sent me back to the Senate for one more term.

Throughout the day, I would field calls from local and statewide media, in between attendance at multiple business, civic, and community events around the state. Harriet and I would get in the car and just drive, and drive, and drive. It would take about two weeks to get all the way around the state—stopping along the way.

Scanning the newspapers and websites in the morning for topical issues that were bubbling locally and nationally, I would then respond to them with at least one press release each week. These short documents, which I drafted myself, would outline my position on a particular issue: The Affordable Care Act and my advocacy for rural cooperatives, or reducing the national debt, or my support of same-sex marriage, or the need for better air service to our state, or my support for a national gas tax, or the state of our aging infrastructure. I was sleeping about three to four hours every night; it was exhausting. Yet it was a renewal of sorts for me because I could sense I was getting traction with voters.

How did I know? Because of the bipartisan voter feedback, I was receiving. In April, I was invited to speak at a Sioux Falls Democrat Forum, a weekly gathering of county Democrat activists who meet for lunch at the local VFW hall. Mostly educators and small business people, a mix of men and women, this group is centrist or moderately liberal on all issues. At this particular meeting, there were about fifty attendees. I spoke to them from the heart, talking about how hard it was to run as an Independent and how much has changed in the two decades since I had last run for office. I told them that, ironically, my campaign in 2014 was very similar to my first campaign in 1974: it was low-budget, homespun, and only focused on the issues. Continuing by citing my moderate views on social issues, I think I surprised them. After all, they were expecting a Republican!

In addition, I told them that, although I served in combat in Vietnam, I was not a defense "hawk." Moreover, I had come to see many of our conflicts overseas as a waste of American blood and treasure. We were not the policemen of the world. I explained that one of my many teaching assignments since leaving the Senate was as a Fulbright professor in Italy. There Harriet and I had observed that we still had forty-four obsolete military installations from World War II. Outlandish and wasteful! These troops should be returned to the United States, perhaps used to secure our southern border at no additional cost to taxpayers— better to spend money at home on education, deficit reduction, senior citizens, roads, and tax relief. I believe our deficit is the largest threat to our economy and our national defense.

After I finished my speech, the men and women in the audience asked me many questions, an indication to me that they were truly engaged. Did I think Vietnam was a mistake? I admitted that I thought it was. What was my position on the Keystone XL Pipeline? I told them that I wasn't against pipelines. I was against the Keystone XL Pipeline *route*. Why? South Dakotans have too little potable drinking water. To route a tar-sands oil pipeline over ninety-two miles of the Ogallala Aquifer, which is the planned route of the Keystone XL Pipeline, is irresponsible. This shallow-water aquifer is located beneath the Great Plains and supplies drinking water to 82 percent of the 2.3 million people who live in the Great Plains, but its depletion is accelerating. Native Americans in my state are worried about this trend. The proposed pipeline route could create an environmental scar across the face of America, and I agree with President Obama's efforts to block it.

The proposed Keystone XL Pipeline could not carry North Dakota oil because the viscosity is so different from the Canadian's tar-sands oil. This issue is a prime example of a big company telling its investors one thing and telling the public the other and getting away with it. Our state should have sought and should still seek two new pipelines from the Bakken oil fields of North Dakota through Minnesota into Chicago. This would move North Dakota oil through a pipeline that would not have to be hauled by train or truck and would not cross a major aquifer. The right-of-way for these pipelines currently exists. Hauling the oil by pipeline is much more environmentally safe than hauling by train or truck.

The Democratic governor of Minnesota has also requested this move to provide relief to the South Dakota grain issue. During my campaign road trips, I saw mountains of grain stacked up all over the state—I had never seen anything like it. They reminded me of Vincent Van Gogh's paintings of golden haystacks in the south of France.

Farmers told me that they had to wait three to six months for an available rail car to transport their grain to market. To alleviate this problem, the government must put pressure on BNSF Railway, which is one of the largest railroad networks in

North America and covers the western two-thirds of the United States. An Independent senator could work out a compromise on this issue that a Republican or a Democrat could not.

Again, none of my opponents in this campaign was offering much detail on the pipeline debate. The Republican was in support of it. The Democrat was against it. But it is a highly nuanced issue that deserved thoughtful consideration— its impact on farmers, business, and national security.

After the lunch, the crowd lined up to shake my hand. A former employee of Democratic Senator Tim Johnson was in the audience and he asked for my autograph. It was ironic, since Senator Johnson was the man who had defeated me in 1996. I had never received such warmth and enthusiasm from Democrats before. I think they appreciated my candor and transparency, and how genuine my intentions were. I sensed a hunger, or yearning, for an Independent.

In my opinion, there are two types of politicians: those who are self-serving and in office to further their career and power, and those who are serving in public office for more altruistic reasons. I hope and pray that I've been the latter. Over the years, I have been offered many opportunities to cash in on my legislative and legal experience—either as a corporate attorney or as a lobbyist.

I was actually offered a lucrative job (in excess of $1 million annually) to help dismantle the 1996 Telecommunications Act, the bill I had worked so hard to pass. Sad to say, it is not uncommon to see formerly elected officials hired to reverse their legislative achievements. Neither the law nor lobbying interested me, although the money was very tempting. I just wanted to continue to find a way to serve the greater good. (When our bank account is low, my wife Harriet reminds me of this road not taken.)

The bottom line was that, although I knew this campaign was going to be a daily struggle, I felt it was my calling and my destiny. I really did. I was energized by the voters and wanted to figure out how to reach as many of them as possible—as efficiently as possible. How could I do that with such a small amount of money and such a geographically large state? Social media and television.

I did not know much about Facebook in 2014 and I definitely didn't know how to use it effectively. So I asked an old friend of mine who has managed a few Facebook campaigns—mostly for nonprofit and community organizations—if he would build and manage my Facebook page as a volunteer. Mike Doan, who is also a retired journalist who spent his career at the Associated Press, *U.S. News & World Report*, and Kiplinger, agreed. He provided some sound, old-school media advice to me as well.

Mike quickly built up a small following on Facebook and recommended that I also buy some targeted ads on the platform. He educated me on its efficiency: for about $200, we could reach everyone in South Dakota who had a Facebook account. It was interesting to me how instantaneous a medium Facebook is and how carefully you have to choose your words in this printed forum. One woman posted a comment: "Would you please get me some signs to put in my yard?" One of our volunteers posted what we thought was a simple and innocent reply, indicating that our low-budget campaign couldn't afford yard signs and that she should make her own. She was deeply offended. Mike had to intervene, apologize, and explain the response. It is hard to convey "tone" on social media, but he was effective at it. The woman ended up being one of our biggest supporters and very active for us on Facebook. It seemed strange to me that this entire exchange took place transparently and online.

During my first campaign in 1974, naturally the Internet and social media did not exist, nor were they a factor in 1996 during my last campaign. To me they were a big, hairy beast that I didn't understand. I knew they could be a powerful publicity venue, but I did not fully comprehend how damaging they could be. Without a team of digital media experts who could perform search engine optimization, manage my online reputation, and do large-scale damage control, I had to trust people like Mike to make it work for me on a severely limited budget. It certainly was cheaper than television ads, but I was frustrated by how easy it was for anonymous strangers to use social media as a megaphone to make false accusations—there were actually fake Larry Pressler Facebook pages with negative and untrue allegations posted about me—and there was nothing I could do about it.

Also vital was a new website, one that would assist my campaign efforts and take donations. My one paid staff member, Colin O'Neal, was responsible for overhauling it. With the help of a software company specializing in campaigns and under the direction of Colin, we relaunched our site, www.larrypressler.com, in June of 2014. Colin updated it daily with our press releases, statements, press coverage, and a listing of my campaign appearances. But he was also my campaign treasurer, so he was stretched. And if he was on the road with me attending an event, we were sometimes a bit delayed in getting the website updated. Limited staff definitely made it difficult to support all the demands of a statewide campaign.

Television ads to reach my voters were crucial, but I didn't know how to produce and place an effective ad campaign on our shoestring budget. South Dakota has two major media markets: Sioux Falls in the eastern part of the state and Rapid City in the west. Almost every resident of South Dakota can be reached in these two television markets.

My goddaughter, Brooke Schieffer, a Vassar University graduate, owns her own Sioux Falls–based advertising agency, Broke Free Productions. I asked her to spearhead my media strategy; because she knew I had a tight budget, she waived her fee. I didn't want to spend our limited resources on consultants and poll-driven media messages. I wanted to get my message out quickly— in a transparent and unfiltered way. Brooke helped me test out an ad that aired in South Dakota during the Oscars in February. The movie *American Hustle* had been nominated for several Academy Awards, and we wanted to capitalize on the surrounding hype. We used an empty television studio with a white background and I read right into the camera, explaining my unique role in the ABSCAM sting popularized by the movie. I also reiterated my pledge to serve only one term, which would make me "free to fight to protect South Dakota families." We thought that if we could have a Senate candidate talking about a popular movie right around the time of the Oscars, we could generate some buzz. Well, we certainly did! The national press immediately picked up on it. By leveraging this unique coincidence, I was able to reintroduce myself very effectively to a statewide audience, and to tie the popularity of this movie to my message. Nobody else had ever seen a campaign tactic like this one.

Chris Matthews was one of the first national network hosts to call me and invite me on his nightly public affairs show, *Hardball*, airing nationwide on MSNBC. Others followed over the next few months. This reaction told me that, despite the conventional wisdom that the presumptive Republican nominee was unbeatable, people really wanted a horserace—not a coronation.

Brooke and I started to work on more ads. Over the course of the summer, in between long road trips to visit voters all over the state, she and I would confer on message, content, timing, and placement. Then Brooke and her company would hire the contractors to produce and place the ads. She gently told me that I looked a bit "wooden" and brittle in the *American Hustle* ad, so we experimented and tried an outdoor setting in casual clothes. The difference was dramatic. I looked more relaxed, confident, and upbeat— because I was.

We next assembled a biographical ad, a two-minute montage of photos from my career that showed me with many historical leaders: former presidents John Kennedy, Richard Nixon, Lyndon Johnson, Jimmy Carter, Ronald Reagan, Bill Clinton, and George Bush; former Cuban president Fidel Castro; and former Egyptian president Hosni Mubarak. We wanted to appeal to those South Dakota Millennial generation voters, who were too young to remember the last time I was the state's U.S. senator. To differentiate me from the other candidates, we described my two decades of experience working for South Dakota and the nation. That worked, too. We started running that ad as soon as it was finished and I got feedback from people on the street telling me that, while they didn't know me before 2014, they were backing me in the upcoming election.

On June 3, the results of the primaries came in and former Governor Mike Rounds, as expected, was the Republican nominee. Rick Weiland, former adviser to Democratic Senator Tim Daschle, won the Democratic primary. The field for the general election was set. Some Republicans were still calling me a spoiler, and most of the media were still not taking my candidacy very seriously.

Later in June, Survey USA, a polling firm that conducts market research for corporations and special-interest groups among more than fifty television stations, released a poll. It indicated that I would get 17 percent of the votes in a four- way race in South Dakota if the election were held at that time. I was gaining on my competitors. This "spoiler" was starting to look a lot more like a "disrupter."

To Senator Larry Pressler
Thanks for the great round of golf,

Bill Clinton

President Bill Clinton and I have been on friendly terms since before our days in public office because of our Rhodes Scholar connection. Photo courtesy of the White House.

I demonstrated my independent streak when I first visited Cuban President Fidel Castro in Havana in 1991, a time when few other politicians and businesses dared. Photo courtesy of Dan Nelson.

CHAPTER 14

Impeachment and a
Groundswell of Support

Impeachment? In late June, South Dakota's Republican Party passed a resolution at their convention calling for the impeachment of President Obama. It was ridiculous. Sponsored by the state's Republican Party activists who had adopted the Tea Party philosophy, the resolution cited the president's controversial exchange of five Taliban prisoners for a U.S. Army sergeant. The hatred for President Obama was brutally apparent. During the party's debate over the resolution, one supporter said: "If anyone in this room cannot see the horrendous, traitorous scandals run by the Obama administration, I will pray for you." I was embarrassed for my former party. I don't agree with all of President Obama's policies, but nothing he has done in office has been impeachable. Very few Republicans objected to the state party's call, which astounded and disappointed me. But it did make international news. One of my former French students even called me about it from Paris. South Dakota made international news—but not for the right reasons.

Therefore, as I did several times a week during the campaign, I issued a strong, independent statement. I put my heart and soul into it, outlining concrete recommendations I believed could make a positive difference on the issue. No platitudes. No personal attacks. Had I been a conventional candidate, I would have been constrained by party leadership and not allowed to do this. I also held two press conferences that week to drive home this message: one in Sioux Falls and one in Rapid City, which required a half day's drive to travel between the two locations.

The message began, "I am inviting President Obama to come to South Dakota to a listening meeting I am sponsoring this fall at Pressler Park in Humboldt, South Dakota [my hometown of 500 people]. We have had two presidents visit Humboldt: George H.W. Bush when he was President, and President Jimmy Carter when he was a candidate."

Part of my declaration was aimed directly at the president:

> Mr. President, I would be proud to appear on the same platform with you. Please be advised that most people, Republicans and Democrats, are embarrassed by this resolution, and we want to tell you that you are always welcome in South Dakota, that we want to work with you during your last two and a half years. Although we may disagree with you on a lot of issues, we admire your steadfast resolve to have an affordable health care program. Mr. President, I supported you in the last two elections for conservative reasons. As I have told you previously, I feared that my friend Senator John McCain would get us into too many foreign wars, and those are very expensive to the U.S. Treasury. As a moderately conservative fiscal person, I believe we must spend far less in foreign wars and spend more domestically on programs such as the Affordable Care Act.

This aggressive stance was not making me popular with the

ardent conservatives in my state. I was a bit defiant, but for a good reason. I'm tired of the slash-and- burn tactics used by the two parties against each other. This is not how our founding fathers envisioned the two parties working. They wanted a healthy tension between the two—one that fosters negotiation and moderation, not extremist views and policies. But this debacle is regrettably what we have today. As a Democratic or Republican politician, you are forced to adopt a uniform set of beliefs and positions that are diametrically opposite from your competitors'. You cannot adopt any middle ground or you are vilified by your party. It's insane. I was determined to place my stake firmly *in the middle*.

Next, I took a costly stand on an issue that probably further alienated me with conservatives: I filed an *amicus curiae* ("Friend of the Court") brief with the U.S. District Courts of South Dakota supporting gay marriage. (I had previously filed one with the U.S. Supreme Court.) An *amicus curiae* is someone who is not a party to a case but offers unsolicited information that might bear on the case. My opinion on this issue has evolved significantly over time, as it has with many people. I arrived at my current belief because of my extensive experience working with military veterans, especially the work I do as a member of the board of directors of the Jericho Homeless Veterans project in New York City. I was an early supporter of gays in the military. Now that they are allowed to serve openly, those who are in committed relationships and are raising children deserve the same rights as heterosexual married couples. South Dakota is home to several large military bases, so there is a practical aspect to this matter. As I write this book, the Supreme Court has just ruled in the case of *Obergefell v. Hodges*, legalizing gay marriage throughout the United States. I'm proud of my small role.

Does it seem like I was beginning to sound like a Democrat? That was the buzz in late June. One of the most senior, experienced, and respected journalists in South Dakota, Bob Mercer, wrote in his government blog that "the presence of former U.S. Senator Larry Pressler in the contest appears to be hurting [Democratic nominee] Weiland much more than [Republican nominee] Rounds."

How so? Mercer went on to explain:

> Pressler is/was a Republican who voted for President Barack Obama, a Democrat, and is running for a return to the Senate as an Independent. Earlier this year we wondered whether Pressler would capture votes from the liberal and moderate Republican voters... The Pressler candidacy, however, seems to be capturing the middle that Weiland hasn't been able to crack. Rounds might or might not reach 50 percent with Pressler and Howie in the race. Howie doesn't affect Weiland, but Pressler does. Weiland might or might not break 35 percent. The question then becomes: Could Pressler get more votes than Rounds if Weiland dropped out of the contest altogether and the Democratic Party didn't replace him? That is the dilemma facing Democrats.

> Would they prefer Pressler or Rounds to be elected in November? Without much of a chance of Weiland beating Rounds, and with the Rounds campaign successfully moving through a five-way primary that was a test run for November, the move that is left for a weak Democratic organization would be to embrace Larry Pressler as the "Independent-Democratic" candidate.

Indeed, there was a groundswell of support for Weiland to

drop out, and for his supporters to embrace me. Unbelievable.

Now I was being considered a potential Democratic spoiler. This campaign was just getting interesting.

CHAPTER 15

State Fair: Reconnecting with South Dakota Voters

W hile I knew early in my campaign that the voter turnout to these midterm elections would be low, I had no idea *how* low. That spring and summer, the media were reporting that less than 25 percent of the Millennials were planning to vote that year.

I saw evidence of this apathy over the course of the summer of 2014 and throughout my campaign. It was disheartening and humbling. Even though I was a seasoned politician and public figure in South Dakota and had received some welcome publicity early on, very few voters or media under the age of thirty-six knew who I was yet. My standard campaign tactics in 1996 involved going to many, many events and tapping into radio and print media outlets where I could have a substantive discussion and not be reduced to a sound bite. Now I realized that many people—especially the young voting bloc I was trying to get to know— don't attend campaign events like they did in the heyday of retail politics. Those few who did follow politics seemed to rely on media—television, the Internet, and social media—to shape their opinions. News radio in most of the small cities and towns in South Dakota (which makes up most of our state) has disappeared, as the small radio stations have been gobbled up by national conglomerates that have centralized their news operations. Hastening their decline, satellite radio has cannibalized the local radio audience.

Gone are the days when I could stop at the state capital in Pierre and meet with a group of political correspondents and wire reporters. The number of reporters covering state and local politics in my state has plummeted over the last few decades, as it has throughout the United States. And everyone knows that printed newspapers are a dying breed. At the same time, online and social media has exploded. As candidates, we now deal with all these so-called "citizen journalists" who can "publish" almost anything on their blogs and Facebook comments—truth, rumor, or downright falsehoods. All of this noise made it an uphill battle for me to get my unfiltered message out to the younger voters.

Accordingly, I went to one of the few events that young people still attend in South Dakota: the state fair. If you want to see American history in person, attend a state fair in the Midwest. And if you want to see the history of South Dakota, attend our state fair. It was first held in Huron in 1885. The legacy of 4-H's involvement in the Fair dates back to 1919. It spreads over 190 acres and has fourteen permanent buildings.

While it is something of a dying tradition, the state fair is still a very large event that attracts a cross-section of South Dakotans—almost 200,000 people annually. After all, agriculture is still South Dakota's number one industry. This institution is truly in my blood. As a boy, the state fair in Huron was my first major trip away from home. As a matter of fact, my family seldom ventured outside the borders of my home county, Minnehaha County, so going to the state fair was a big and exciting deal. I stayed in the 4-H men's dorm, which housed about thirty to forty young men in bunk beds. Sometime after the lights were out, about 10:00 p.m., there would be an informal, storytelling contest in the dark. Some of our jokes had a real rural flavor to them: "What if you cross a purebred, Spotted Poland-China hog with an

Angus cow?" The answer to the question was a Hereford cow, much to the chagrin of the Hereford owners!

At the state fair and at other major county fairs throughout South Dakota that summer of 2014, I had a routine. I rose early, put on a pair of jeans and a blue shirt and maybe a baseball cap, and I walked the entire fairgrounds by myself at least twice a day—averaging four to five miles. I carried little campaign cards in my pocket and walked through the cattle and hog barns, as well as the industrial and machinery exhibits, passing out my cards. I greeted the livestock owners, 4-Hers, the fair goers, and the fair employees. At the risk of sounding self-serving, I still do have a substantial knowledge of all hog, sheep, and cattle breeds, as well as in-depth knowledge of all the hybrid seed varieties. So I could converse at the fair with the most detailed expertise. Believe it or not, I still know many of the breeders and their families from my days in 4-H, although there are fewer of them now. As a former 4-H judge myself, I was asked by an alert judge to give my views on the class of hogs being judged. I chose the top four hogs in the class and gave my reasons: "Look for a deep ham with a strong arching back and a trim jowl." I received a round of applause from the audience.

The agricultural industry has changed: purebred breeders of cattle, hogs, and sheep now use public relations firms, the Internet, and a scientific—or mathematical— approach to advertise and sell their animals. Purebred hogs are no longer brought to the state fair because of the risk of spreading disease. This has reduced the number of attendees. Also, now that schools start as early as mid- August, many of the 4-H students are precluded from participating. That has hurt fair attendance as well. There are many who advocate for an earlier state fair, but that is almost impossible because the livestock are not yet mature enough. The Millennial-aged voters who do attend the fair seem to be more attracted to the country western and bluegrass concerts. I couldn't compete with that entertainment.

The fast food available at these fairs is universally bad. Ironically, there are no fresh fruits and vegetables to buy for eating there—or any lean pork or beef, for that matter, although that is the criterion on which the fair's blue-ribbon winners are determined. I always tried to bring some fruit with me and I would take a break and eat lunch—by myself in a picnic area. People would frequently stop and talk to me about some particular interest they had, or out of sheer curiosity about my Independent campaign. I did not have paid staff with me, so I was not able to capture the contact information of the people I met. If I had taken a paid staffer with me (as I used to do when I was a Republican serving in the Senate), I probably could have converted some of them into campaign contributors. That is one of the problems with running as an Independent with a largely volunteer staff.

As I walked around, I would also be insulted a few times every day by people who just didn't like politicians. Did it bother me? After less than two decades as an elected official, I have learned to have a tough skin and not to take it too personally. It's just part of the deal you make with yourself when you volunteer for this life. But it is also the reason why many high-quality, fine people will not run for public office. They simply don't want the abuse.

One of the things I like to check out at state fairs is the farming equipment. I am an old tractor fan, and I like to see the new equipment. I can still recognize them, but they now seem to resemble equipment for construction rather than for farming. I don't have the personal, emotional identification with these new types of tractors as I did with the older models.

Back when I was growing up, tractors were simpler and they actually had personalities that stemmed from their idiosyncrasies. In fact, it was almost as though the farmer's and his tractor's personalities merged. Farmers become attracted to either the "red" line of tractors or the "green" line of tractors. The reds are International Harvesters (Farmalls) and the greens are John Deeres.

Attending the fairs gave me an advantage because I could talk and relate to *any* of the farmers or dealers about their business: they knew I was one of them. That made a difference. This version of old-fashioned, retail politics is my favorite type. But realistically it was very hard to meet enough people to make a real dent in public opinion— especially when I was about to face a deluge of negative advertising in the coming weeks. I could not have ever predicted what a battering I was about to endure.

CHAPTER 16

Gun Control and Immigrants

L ate summer 2014 was an ideal time for a candidate like me to spend time forging strong constituency relationships and issuing concrete opinions on substantive issues I knew were relevant to South Dakotans. I had to be out in public every day, meeting the voters. In contrast, my opponents were only issuing their parties' meaningless slogans—echoing whatever their party leadership wanted them to say. The Republican candidate was saying: "Repeal Obamacare!" (Oddly enough, the Republicans have been totally silent on repealing Obamacare since the election.) The Democratic candidate was saying: "Tell the billionaires and special interests they can't buy South Dakota!" This was ridiculous and hypocritical, since the Democrat was taking more corporate money—on a percentage basis—than any politician in South Dakota's history. The incendiary comments of both candidates just fed into the fears of the voters.

Traveling around the state, logging many miles and attending multiple events per day, my goal was to interact in person with as many voters as possible and present my argument for more Independents in the U.S. Senate. I would tell them how South Dakota could make history by creating this unprecedented Independent voting bloc. Most people I took the time to educate on this concept became enthusiasts, but I knew that getting the necessary volume of people to hear and vote for this message was near impossible. The fall campaign season, the eight weeks between Labor Day and November 4, was just around the corner. It would be a mad dash to the finish line!

I chose some very small towns in the state to make some campaign speeches about two controversial issues: gun control and immigration. Speaking in the northeastern quadrant of my state at the community center in Tulare— with a population of 500 people, and at the Best Western hotel in Huron—with a population of 13,000, I reiterated my support for stronger background checks. Contrary to popular belief, people in small towns like these actually seem to accept stronger background checks.

South Dakota has some of the least restrictive gun laws in the nation—no requirements for a permit to purchase a handgun, a shotgun, or a rifle. Since 2009, anyone who passes a federal background check can immediately take possession of any firearm in South Dakota. Most conservative South Dakota pheasant hunters (including me) support stronger background checks on guns—especially to prevent mentally ill people from obtaining guns.

A recent survey in South Dakota indicates that nearly 50 percent of our state's residents support a background check. I believe, and I said this at the time, that the National Rifle Association (NRA) and some of the gun control special- interest groups are a paper tiger in the general election. In Republican primaries, the NRA can have a great influence. But I believe that, if we can get this issue into a general election, we will find that most reasonable people do support background checks.

We've had too many school shootings by people with mental illness, and we need to better protect the public's safety. I believe this has become a conservative position, because it will help to preserve the gun rights of hunters and other law-abiding, sane citizens who wish to have guns.

Immigration was another hot-button issue. At campaign speeches in Yankton and at the Turner County Fair in Parker—

both small, historic towns in the southeastern corner of the state—I reiterated my specific immigration reform plan, which I also presented on a local radio show the evening before. I recommended that we: (1) relocate U.S. troops from obsolete foreign bases and place them on the southern border of Texas and Arizona; that would secure our southern border at no extra cost to the U.S. government and taxpayers, because we are already paying those troops; (2) institute a path to citizenship as proposed by Presidents George W. Bush and Barack Obama; and (3) ensure that this path to citizenship included a background check so that no criminals or drug dealers could remain in the country.

As I have said many times, we need immigrants. We are a country of immigrants—our economy depends on them. Over the years, I have personally helped more than twenty- five Vietnamese families legally emigrate to the U.S. I also support an expanded work visa program. However, our border is a sieve and it attracts illegal immigrants in large numbers. We must secure our border, and immigrants must enter the country legally. We should not allow children to be sent across the border in the future. Many of these children are sent here without their parents to circumvent the legal intent of the law. It's heartbreaking, and terribly dangerous for the children.

Running as an Independent, I was at last free to express my innermost convictions on these two issues. Had I been on the GOP or the Democratic ticket, I would have been forced to follow a script in order to receive campaign money.

"Strongly opposed!" That was my position on the proposed merger of Comcast and Time Warner. I've always been a Teddy Roosevelt, trust-busting kind of politician. Again, I distributed an issues-oriented statement about my opposition. I was worried about the adverse effect this merger might have on RFD-TV, a cable channel aimed at rural America. I am a fan of RFD-TV because of its programs on cattle-raising, old tractors, horsemanship, grain prices, seed technology, and country music. It was educational and entertaining for my state's primary industry.

Many South Dakotans watch RFD-TV on satellite dishes and on some cable channels. What happens with these giant mergers is that useful programming, like that on RFD-TV, is frequently replaced with superficial programming that does not fit our rural, small-town needs. At the time, I sent a private letter to the Federal Communications Commission (FCC) urging that the merger not be approved, and if it was, that RFD-TV be kept on the air. I was satisfied to learn that the merger was terminated in April 2015.

In late August, I accepted an invitation to participate in a Senate debate on September 10 sponsored by KSFY-TV. At the time, I estimated that we had lost the opportunity to have approximately five debates because the Republican and/or Democratic nominees refused to participate. Independent candidates depend on these debates to get out their message. In my last campaign in 1996, I had agreed to nine electronic, radio, or TV debates. It's clear that the real debating tradition is dying out both in South Dakota and nationwide. Today's campaign debates are limited to one hour for four candidates, which results in each candidate speaking for only about ten to twelve minutes.

I felt like the lone participant—or lone *willing* participant— in many of the proposed debates during this time. In fact, campaigning in the late summer of 2014 in rural South Dakota was a lonely venture. Frequently on the campaign trail by myself, I couldn't tap into the local support that a party candidate can. It was part of the double-edged sword of running as an Independent: I had the freedom to dictate my schedule and my message with no political party oversight, but I had very little help. While I wasn't lonely because the voters energized me, I was definitely on my own.

CHAPTER 17

Threading the Needle:
Finding Walter Cronkite

In most political campaigns, conventional wisdom dictates that you wait until after Labor Day to spend the majority of your budget. After all, why spend a lot of money on advertising in the spring and summer, when most voters are not even focused on elections until a few weeks—or even a few days—before the election? The theory is that you concentrate your spending at the end of the election season to maximize your exposure and, hopefully, significantly increase your awareness and support among target voters.

We decided to do the opposite. I knew I had *one* chance to "thread the needle" and build a surge of interest and support—*before* my opponents. I decided to spend what little money I had on four weeks of television advertising in late August and early September, typically a slow month for political advertising. We wanted to get people talking and to appear competitive—even if my poll numbers weren't actually there yet. That way, we might be able to attract some money and support from outside the state. The key was to have ads that differentiated me and my message. They needed to be a bit unconventional.

Once again, I relied on Brooke Schieffer and Broke Free Productions to help me produce my ads. She wanted to get creative, and she started brainstorming. She remembered a story about Walter Cronkite, where he had said some nice things about me on the air right after the ABSCAM scandal hit the news. Off the air, he told me that he wished he could live in a state where he could vote for me. His candor was extraordinary. She wondered if we could we find a copy of his old newscast.

Brooke and her team scoured the Internet for this now-ancient video clip. Even in the Internet age, it was like looking for a needle in a haystack! They found it at the Vanderbilt University library—a 56-second clip of Walter Cronkite praising me on the air. Brooke showed it to Harriet and me, and it made Harriet cry. I knew it was good stuff, so we turned it into a 60-second ad that opened with the now- familiar reference to the *American Hustle* movie—to give it currency. Next came a clip of the sting operation where I clearly turned down the bribe. Finally, we showed a clip of Walter Cronkite broadcasting my original quote: "I turned down an illegal contribution. Whatever have we come to if that is considered heroic?" At the time, Cronkite's coverage put me in the national spotlight for several weeks.

We led with this ad, and it got people talking. They stopped me on the street, telling me how Walter Cronkite's compliments impressed them. Then Brooke helped me produce an ad that was intended to show how I have worked, and intended to work, with both political parties. We wanted the ad to show the personal friendships and working relationships that I developed with Presidents Reagan and Clinton. Again, Brooke used an outdoor background and dressed me more casually. She had me speak directly into the camera and tell the audience, "I believe in taking the best ideas from both parties. I was a strong supporter of Ronald Reagan when it came to our nation's freedom, but I stood with President Clinton for fiscally conservative, balanced budgets. I'm as independent as South Dakota, and I will use my seniority to be a game changer for ending the partisan gridlock." Brooke made me look like a statesman.

The ads aired in the Sioux Falls and Rapid City television media markets. For those four weeks, I outspent my Republican challenger. In addition, my campaign matched my Democratic challenger in television gross rating points (GRPs) for the 35+ age demographic in both media markets. Brooke and her company developed my media plan for the rest of the campaign. Based upon the contributions of South Dakotans and my personal loans to the campaign, we felt we could air a comprehensive television ad campaign between August and the first week of November. In the end, my advertising campaign was insignificant against the onslaught of advertising targeted to defeat me. At the time, however, we were operating without the benefit of campaign-financed polls, surveys, focus groups, and testing. Running as an Independent does not afford you that kind of luxury! Indeed, we were operating on sheer political instinct.

While I was busy saturating the airwaves during August, my competitors were doing...nothing. The Republican nominee had seemed to "go dark" during that time frame. In effect, I was advertising in the clear. This situation helped me to gain traction without any competitive clutter and it gave me a significant headwind as we shifted into the busy fall campaign season. We wanted to prove that no party had a monopoly on all the answers.

Indeed, a poll released on September 9 by Survey USA showed that my support had jumped to 25 percent. The same survey showed both of my opponents falling: the Republican nominee to 39 percent, and the Democratic nominee to 28 percent. One opponent had spent more than $3 million; another had spent more than $800,000. Their messages? More partisan bickering. My campaign had spent less than $80,000 on television. My message? Detailed, meaningful opinions on issues that have real impact on South Dakotans. We need more Independents to make that kind of impact in Washington.

At the time, the founder of Survey USA stated that the poll

was "resonant of the election in Kansas, to this extent, which is there are more voters in the state voting against the Republican than voting for the Republican. In the Kansas Senate race, the Democratic nominee withdrew from the contest, leaving Independent candidate Greg Orman in a competitive race which had previously been predicted an easy Republican victory." South Dakota was also expected to be an easy Republican victory. But with the Republicans and Democrats busy tearing each other down in Kansas and South Dakota, neither party was paying attention to Independents like Greg Orman and me. That was about to change.

CHAPTER 18

On Fire!

"The Pressler campaign is on fire!" My campaign chairman, Don Frankenfeld, minced no words in response to the September 9 poll numbers. It really was a validation of what Harriet and I had been feeling intuitively and hearing as we traveled across the state. The people were reacting to my intensely personal, issues-oriented campaign, and I was on a trajectory to victory. I was in it to win it!

That night, I appeared in a live debate hosted by KSFY- TV of Sioux Falls. It was simulcast nationally on C-SPAN. My Republican opponent refused to participate. The Democratic candidate spent most of the debate criticizing our Republican opponent. In contrast, I talked about specific actions I would take as a newly elected senator. I also tried to communicate how effective a small group of Independent senators could be in breaking the poisonous deadlock in Washington. Since my opponents were bickering like toddlers, I seemed to transcend their pandering.

Even though I could only speak for sixty seconds at a time, I felt confident with my performance. I kept a small set of notes on 3 x 5 index cards for every debate. Each card listed one of the three key themes of my life: idealism, spirituality, and service. But "idealism" topped the first card every time and I pounded away at this theme in every debate. What did I mean by "idealism"? Idealism meant that I was running a campaign based on ideals and ideas. The ideals were my bedrock values of honesty and integrity. The ideas were my proposals on specific issues facing South Dakotans and the nation.

Vernon Brown, the KSFY senior political reporter, seemed to agree. Afterward, he said on air, "I think, if we're going to gauge it by points, I think Pressler got the most points, probably because he was the only one that spelled out his background, told us his experience—everything from growing up on a farm by Humboldt to his time in Vietnam, being a Rhodes Scholar, and his twenty-two years of Congress. We learned about his past. We don't know, based on that hour tonight, much about the qualifications of the other two that were present."

Brown seemed to like what he saw: "You know I covered him in his '96 campaign, where he lost, and it seems like a different Larry Pressler. There's more clarity, he told me he's having more fun. He's not handcuffed by being part of a party, so he can really talk about what he believes. I think we're seeing him be more independent in that sense as well." Indeed, in almost every debate forum (and I participated in about twelve), I was declared the "winner" and was deemed "senatorial."

Brown was right—I was having more fun. I was energized by the voters and buoyed by my ascendancy. The next day, I headed out with Harriet on a fifteen-city tour of the majestic, mountainous Black Hills region of the state. Once again, she drove. We made stops in Rapid City, Wall, Deadwood, Lead, Bison, McIntosh, McLaughlin, Mobridge, Webster, Selby, Hartford, Aberdeen, Sisseton-Wahpeton, Milbank, and Sioux Falls. We participated in a Native American debate sponsored by the *Native Sun News* and United Tribes Technical College in Rapid City; an independent candidate forum sponsored by the South Dakota Voice of Independents—also in Rapid City; walked the streets and cafés in Deadwood and Lead, including the Deadwood casinos; attended the National Association of Retired

Federal Employees (NARFE) Candidate's Forum in Aberdeen; and met with Sisseton-Wahpeton tribal leaders in the Roberts County area. September was a blur of activity!

One particularly memorable visit during that two-week tour was to Bison High School in Bison, a small town north of Rapid City in the northwestern quadrant of the state. An old frontier town, Bison has a long history of ranching and farming. In fact, the library there houses a sizable collection of frontier memorabilia. This "museum" is only open when the librarian turns on the lights for visitors. The population of Bison is fewer than 500 people, so its school draws from small towns all over the county. It is not unusual for students to commute thirty minutes or more to get to school. This school has a good reputation and routinely sends some of its graduates to Ivy League schools. The town's population is more than 95 percent white, and the median household income is $30,000.

As the town still relies on farming and ranching for its livelihood, the school's stated mission includes fostering pride in its rural community. We were invited by the school's twelfth-grade civics teacher, who turned out the entire student body to attend the event. Almost 150 students assembled in the school auditorium to hear my talk. The kids were very respectful and dressed up for the event. I was not surprised at how many questions focused on the cost of higher education, given how small their families' household incomes were. Afterward, they served us home-baked cookies and fresh lemonade. It was classic, small-town South Dakota and it reminded me of what mine looked like in the 1950s.

The MSNBC talk show *Up with Steve Kornacki* invited me to New York City to be a guest that same week. Steve asked me to comment on ISIS (Islamic State of Iraq and Syria), the Islamic extremist militant group that currently has control over territory in those countries. I told him that I had been a strong opponent of the Iraq war, that I believed ISIS sprang from that war, and that my Vietnam experience made me very hesitant to send in ground troops to fight.

I also took the opportunity to report on my campaign's progress. I said that we were on track to win the three-way race, and said that my main objective was to get back into the U.S. Senate to accomplish some specific legislative goals. One of those goals was to get Congress to actually vote on issues rather than simply pass continuing resolutions: "Congress may have some votes, but they are afraid to pass any resolutions in an election year. I'm running for the Senate in part because on all key issues, Congress delays and pontificates and doesn't take any real action. Congress does this all the time rather than meeting its responsibilities." And the situation remains ridiculous. They claim to make progress when they are really just stalling. A group of Independents is what's needed to break the deadlock on deficit spending, among other issues.

Back in South Dakota, the media were beginning to recognize my unexpected ascendancy in the polls. Bob Mercer, the columnist who had written very favorably about me in June, published an editorial that ran in several South Dakota newspapers and on numerous websites over that weekend in mid-September. He called me the "big surprise" in the 2014 race and pointed out my unusual appeal. Most political forecasters had been predicting that I would only "spoil" the Republicans' support. By Mercer's analysis, I seemed to be taking support away from *both* Republican and Democratic voters: "Scratch the [September 9] survey results a little deeper and you find two points of interest. [Republican nominee] Rounds [and] [Democratic] Weiland ...are essentially one-party candidates, while Pressler has support across the spectrum." Surprising, indeed!

The news just kept getting better and better. Soon after I participated in a debate sponsored by Publisher Giago's *Native*

Sun News, he endorsed me—the first of numerous high-profile and influential endorsements I received over the next few weeks. In his announcement in a *Huffington Post* editorial, Giago said, "I believe the only way Democrats or Independents can stop the Mike Rounds Express is to throw all of their support behind Larry Pressler." He went on to emphasize two key points for his constituents: "Pressler is making some impressive inroads on the Indian reservations. If he is elected, he will bring seniority to his Senate seat because the three terms he served in the Senate will be counted." I was thrilled and grateful for Publisher Giago's kind words and endorsement. I pledged to continue to work hard on all the Indian reservations to earn their support.

People took note of how positive and constructive my campaign was. As the *Rapid City Journal* wrote at the time, "In this year's U.S. Senate race, Rounds is the GOP candidate who is the frontrunner, and he and Democrat Rick Weiland are assailing one another with charges and counter-charges in a series of increasingly negative ads. Meanwhile, Pressler, an independent, is taking the high road and mainly running ads about himself, his positions and his record of integrity."

Certainly I appeared to be picking up a lot of steam—this race was suddenly all about *me*. Political commentators continued to debate whether I was siphoning support from the Republican or the Democrat. When asked about my insurgent campaign, representatives from both candidates' camps continued to attack each other, not me. As I headed into the last four weeks of the campaign, I wondered: How long would this last?

CHAPTER 19

Rabbit in a Firing Range

CNN's Dana Bash traveled from Washington to South Dakota to attend several campaign events—including my cowboy poetry reading, held in a loud and boisterous sports bar/restaurant in mid-October. She was one of several reporters who traveled to cover this event. *The Times* of London even sent a correspondent across the pond to write a story about me.

CNN's Bash called it "an off-beat event befitting an unusual candidacy." (Much later, she told me this event was her favorite of the entire 2014 election season.) But it made sense to me. Cowboy poetry grew out of the campfire tradition of storytelling and singing songs about ranch and farm life, but some of the poetry's messages also reflected those of my campaign.

That evening, in front of a crowd of about fifty people with televisions blaring in the background, I read one of my favorite lines from one of my favorite poems. It was written by the western poet Baxter Black and is called "Take Care of Yer Friends": "A hug or a shake or whatever feels right./It's a highpoint of giving, I'll tell you tonight./All worldly riches and tributes of men/can't hold a candle to the worth of a friend." Indeed! As I said that night and many times on the campaign trail, I've been accused of cavorting with the enemy just because I said that President Obama is a personal friend of mine. What's wrong with that? Why can't Republicans have friends who are Democrats? That's how you get things done in Washington. So many politicians have forgotten that fundamental truth.

CNN's Dana Bash conducted a live interview with me during my poetry reading in Sioux Falls in October. Photo courtesy of Colin O'Neal.

As a member of the Badger Clark Poetry Society, I enjoy these poetry reading events on a regular basis. Badger Clark, known as a cowboy poet, was the Poet Laureate of South Dakota in the 1930s. He read to President Calvin Coolidge in his "summer White House" in Custer, South Dakota. At this campaign event, I also read the classic "Homecoming Queen" by M. J. McMillan, about a pretty young girl with promise who becomes a bitter waitress by the time she is forty: "Waitin' tables and cryin' the blues./Don't judge her too harshly till you've had the chance to walk a few miles in her shoes."

South Dakota poet McMillan was actually in the audience that night. So was the GOP "tracker"—a guy named Nick, who was videotaping my event. He was a bit of a stalker, and he was everywhere, even frightening some of the women volunteering for me. These trackers have a strange job. They are employed by an opposing political party to follow a candidate's campaign, documenting every moment, stirring up mischief, and looking for gaffes or slipups that they can exploit. Politics has become such a rough, mafia-like business that trackers like these are common. In this campaign, he was hired by the GOP to follow me. Dana Bash actually Tweeted about it that night, noting that this political tracker was first following the Democratic candidate. The fact that he was following me meant that I was now on the GOP's hit list. Turned out I was actually in the bull's eye!

It didn't take long for the national political party operatives and the special-interest groups from around the country to start invading South Dakota. When they got a whiff of my surge in the polls, they got scared. They descended on my state. The barrage began.

Within thirty-six hours of the October 8 poll publication, the first attack ads appeared on television and radio. My campaign expected some of this, but we could never have imagined the number, the severity, the inaccuracies, the hate, and the spitefulness of the attacks. Usually, a candidate is attacked by the left *or* the right. I was attacked by *both. It was an ugly blitzkrieg.*

That week, the Weiland campaign, pro-Weiland third-party groups, and the Democratic Party bought 59 percent of all political advertising spots in the state. (A "spot" is the term used to describe advertising space, usually 30 or 60 seconds long.) The Republican Party bought 19 percent of the spots. Outside groups bought 7 percent of the spots. Most of this ad space was filled up with ads from both parties and independent groups attacking me. The *Rapid City Journal* published Federal Election Commission (FEC) data showing that, as of October 17, outside groups had spent $462,529 for the Democratic senatorial candidate, $428,000 for the Republican candidate, and $0 for me. In contrast, outside groups had spent more than $358,327 *against me*, and that number shot up to more than $2 million by the end of the campaign. That is a whole lot of money in tiny South Dakota, and much, much more was spent and reported after the campaign.

These are just some of the outside groups whose spending to defeat me in the 2014 election was recorded to the FEC:

- Americans for Prosperity—funded by the conservative Koch brothers
- Focus on the Family—funded by conservative Charles Dobson
- Progressive Change Campaign Committee—funded by progressive Senator Elizabeth Warren
- Every Voice Action—funded by the liberal father and son George and Jonathan Soros
- National Republican Senatorial Committee—led by conservative Senator Jerry Moran
- National Democratic Senatorial Committee—led by liberal Senator Michael Bennet
- National Rifle Association Political Victory Fund—led by conservative Wayne LaPierre
- National Rifle Association Institute for Legislative Action— also led by Wayne LaPierre
- Democracy for America—led by former Democratic National Committee Chairman and presidential candidate Howard Dean
- 350.org Action Fund—liberal group
- MoveOn.org Political Action—liberal group
- Mayday PAC—led by liberal Lawrence Lessig
- Planned Parenthood of Minnesota Action Fund
- Rushmore PAC—conservative group
- American Chemistry Council, Inc.

- American Hospital Association
- CitizenLink
- Credit Union Legislative Action Council (CULAC)
- Independent Insurance Agents and Brokers of America, Inc.
- National Right to Life Political Action Committee
- National Right to Life Victory Fund
- Blue America PAC Independent Expenditure Committee
- Progressive Kick (PAC) Independent Expenditures
- Many True Conservatives PAC

Although all these groups (outside the two parties and outside South Dakota) were spending money to defeat me, some of them had supported my past campaigns. Yet none of these groups supported me in 2014—how could that be? I think I scared the heck out of them! What these groups are really afraid of having is a real Independent in the Senate. It would upset the whole apple cart.

Each group doubled or tripled their spending before the end of the campaign. Their sole objective was to defeat Independent Larry Pressler. They cared nothing about my philosophy or where I stood. They just did not want another real Independent in the U.S. Senate. Very few of these groups have connections to South Dakota, nor do they care about South Dakotans and the real issues my state faces. They simply wanted to preserve their respective party's numbers in the Senate. Period.

Along with the negative attack ads, money was also spent on attack mailings and robocalls. Lots of them: from liberal groups saying I would raise the eligibility age for Social Security, from conservative groups saying I would "uphold Washington's health care takeover" and calling me a supporter of the "extreme Obamacare agenda," and from conservative groups who left flyers on cars in Catholic church parking lots telling parishioners to "vote for the candidate who will stand on the side of South Dakota values." (That mailer alleged that I was siding "with West Coast liberals," not South Dakota families, in my support of same-sex marriage). Also there were mailers from liberal groups saying that I couldn't be trusted on the issue of abortion and a woman's right to choose.

Then there were the mailers from the GOP quoting me as saying that I was a "friend of Obama's." They were right. Also, there were mailers saying that I was a friend of Mitt Romney's because I donated to his 2012 campaign. They were right, too. People couldn't understand how I could be friendly with both of them. *That's what voters should want in a politician—a representative who can work with everyone!*

Targeting supporters of the Keystone XL oil pipeline were mailers saying I was against it, but they failed to mention that I supported an alternative pipeline. Mailers targeted to environmentalists said I supported the extraction and shipping of North Dakota oil through the Keystone XL Pipeline. All of the allegations in these mailers were complete distortions of my positions and record. Facts didn't seem to pertain.

The GOP and the Democrats have powerfully entrenched special-interest groups that support them. In this campaign, they were deployed into action. I received calls from friends who said they received conflicting mailings—on the same day—from the NRA and gun control groups. One mailer said I planned to *give* everyone guns. The next mailer, allegedly from a local pheasant and duck hunters' association but in reality produced by the NRA, said I planned to *take away* everyone's guns. It was a constant armada of false attacks. I felt like a rabbit in a firing range—with shots coming from all sides and every angle.

And then there were the strange, ghostly spam emails. Thousands of them started flooding my email inbox starting in mid-October and they jammed my server, essentially shutting down my service for two weeks. Big campaigns have the money to disable smaller opponents in this way. The content was identical in each one, mean-spirited, and personally invasive. For example, one subject line read: "Please don't play spoiler. Drop out." Other messages said I was too old to run or that my campaign finance reports were inaccurate or that a personal scandal about me was about to be revealed. Each one was signed by a different person. It was creepy. I suspect the people were fictitious and computer-generated. But given the fact that they all had identical content, I knew there was some campaign entity creating and disseminating them. Without significant technical support, I could not respond adequately.

And with a total budget of $450,000, I was very limited in my ability to strike back. By contrast, my Republican and Democrat opponents' media budgets for one week were $500,000 each. They could afford to saturate the airwaves, and they did. I tried to convince the South Dakota media to analyze all these attack ads and mailers to assess their accuracy. Media in large metropolitan areas (and national media) will dedicate reporters to fact-check national campaign assertions, giving them a "Pinocchio test." In South Dakota, the media wouldn't do that because they had too few political reporters; they told me to do the analysis myself and buy more ads. I had no money to do that, and, frankly, a response ad would have just repeated the negative. While I was disappointed that the people of South Dakota bought into all these negative ads, most reasonable people could see that they were distorted and unfair. Still, I had expected more from the voters. Why doesn't the average citizen put more effort into learning about their political candidates?

Independents rarely receive the campaign "lift" that big outside groups can provide late in the campaign. In fact, the established system works against us. When I sought to march in the South Dakota State University homecoming parade, the largest parade in South Dakota, I was denied entry. This was the first time there was coverage in the local press that I was being treated unfairly. I couldn't find a sponsor. Since I was not a Republican or a Democratic candidate, neither the College Republicans nor the College Democrats would sponsor me. Since I was not a sitting member of Congress, I couldn't qualify as a "dignitary" for the parade. I was caught in limbo and was told I was excluded from riding my 1929 D John Deere tractor—always an attraction in parades.

That's when the South Dakota Farmers Union Collegiate Club at SDSU came to the rescue. Because I was a longtime member of the Farmers Union, the club sponsored me as *their* dignitary in the parade. I was most appreciative.

Despite these challenges, I was still racking up endorsements almost on a daily basis. The retired FBI agent who had led the ABSCAM "sting" operation, John Good, came out of the blue to publicly endorse me. We were put in touch by a *Washington Post* reporter who was doing a story about the movie *American Hustle* and the renewed interest in the ABSCAM scandal, and who quoted both of us in the article. At the height of his career, FBI Agent Good was the highest nonpolitical appointee in the anticorruption division of the Justice Department. He is now retired and living in New York. I had received an email from him saying he was a great admirer. When I called him in early 2014, he said that he wanted to campaign for me as a volunteer.

Unfortunately, Agent Good was in poor health at the time; he was only able to come to South Dakota for a few days in October. He made one campaign event appearance with me and then met with the media, where he said, "When the hidden cameras were running, and $50,000 in cash was ready for a bribe, at a moment when Senator Pressler thought no one on the outside was looking, we saw his true character... At a time when attack ads from extremists on both sides of the aisle are attacking Senator Pressler's integrity, I had to do what I could to tell anyone who will listen that Senator Pressler is an honest politician, and there aren't many of them around."

Agent Good continued: "The only way this country is ever going to recover from the disastrous gridlock taking place now is to get people like Pressler in there. I am 100% behind Pressler. I would do anything for him." I was delighted to have this honest public servant stand with me.

Driving in the South Dakota State University homecoming parade on my "D" John Deere tractor. Photo courtesy of Myles Bialas.

Angus King, the Independent senator from Maine, announced on October 28 that he was supporting me. He said, "I proudly endorse Larry Pressler to serve in the United States Senate as an Independent who will build bridges between Democrats and Republicans... Larry doesn't need this job; he's seeking it as a true patriot who wants to help his state and country in a tough time."

King went on to say that an Independent can be very influential in the Senate: "I want to assure the people of South Dakota that in my first-hand experience, an Independent can be effective in the Senate—by working across the aisle and finding areas of common ground." I consider Senator King one of the most powerful and influential senators in the Senate today. He has a reputation as a fiscal conservative and he was a highly-respected former governor of Maine. It was a great honor to be endorsed by him.

On November 1, my state's largest-circulation newspaper, the *Sioux Falls Argus Leader*, endorsed me. In their editorial, they analyzed each candidate's world views, negotiating skills, aspirational goals, and their openness and honesty. Each of my opponents fell short in one or more category, in their opinion. "And so, we turn to Larry Pressler, a former Republican senator, running as an independent, in a low-key campaign focused on issues and integrity," the editorial staff wrote:

> He has verbalized an international strategy on battling ISIS and fighting Ebola and has serious reservations about sending ground troops into Middle Eastern countries. He has experience in Congress— twenty-two years as a South Dakota representative and senator—and recognizes the seismic partisan shift that has occurred in the years since he left office. As an independent, he talks about working with both parties, which he would be in a position to do.
>
> He has ideas on programs for veterans, on tax reform and debt reduction and is a good communicator. He has promised to serve just one term.

Pressler certainly does not have all the answers. We realize that as a former office holder, he has a record which reflects votes that contradict some positions he now says he holds. While serving in the Senate, Pressler also was criticized for being aloof and less than engaged in the serious issues of the time.

But we think Pressler's approach and outlook have matured. He professes a middle-of-the-road, moderately conservative political philosophy that we think is in line with the bulk of South Dakotans.

When we use our checklist to evaluate the candidates, Larry Pressler comes out on top.

We urge you to outline your expectations for our next senator. And we think you, too, might decide Pressler is the best fit for South Dakota at this time.

Over the next few critical days before the election, the *Rapid City Journal*, the *Mitchell Daily Republic*, and the state's largest Native American newspaper, the *Native Sun News*, endorsed me. It was a clean sweep of all the major newspapers in my state!

Finally, a late campaign surprise: crusty South Dakota media legend Steve Hemmingsen publicly endorsed me. He had never spoken favorably about *any* politician before. Now retired, he was the anchor at Sioux Falls' CBS affiliate and the largest statewide television station, KELO-TV, for thirty years. In a television ad we aired, he said: "I brought you the news for more than thirty years. I have never endorsed a major political candidate before, but the time is at hand. And I back Independent Larry Pressler for U.S. Senate. The gridlock in Washington has gone on long enough, and Larry Pressler, as an Independent U.S.

senator, could be a major wedge in breaking that two-party logjam. Vote for Larry Pressler."

Despite all this good news, I feared that the repeated attacks against me coming from all sides were crowding out my very positive message and my very productive campaign. The drumbeat of negative ads seemed to be quickening—with no balanced response.

On the eve of the election, I watched with disgust as major false, negative ads appeared on television almost every fifteen minutes, accusing me of not supporting Social Security or some other distorted and untrue allegation. The ads were broadcasting outright lies about my positions and deceiving the voters. This is why good people don't run for office. As I went to bed that night, I prayed that the citizens of South Dakota would look past this obnoxious clutter and make rational decisions in the voting booth the next day.

CHAPTER 20

Election Day

Election Days are always nerve-racking for most candidates. You keep thinking that there is more you can do to reach more voters, and convince more of them to vote for you. In today's world of very low voter turnout, you are also just convincing them of the importance of voting— for anyone! On November 4, I issued a press release outlining my Election Day activities in the Sioux Falls area: holding signs with some of my volunteers both in downtown Brandon during morning rush hour, and at two major intersections in Sioux Falls during the afternoon and evening rush hour traffic.

I also told the media that I would be available for interviews that evening by phone from my farm home near Humboldt, and that supporters would be gathering for parties at restaurants in Sioux Falls, Rapid City, and Aberdeen. The parties were "no-host," of course—I was out of money and had run personal debt in excess of $450,000. I had to pay off this debt with my retirement fund, and it was a big hit. If I had been running as a party candidate, my party would almost certainly have helped me pay it off.

My mood that day was bittersweet. The truth was that my campaign had probably been lost over the prior few weeks in the wake of the bombardment from all sides. I was probably doomed from the day I surged in the polls. The political parties' leadership just could not take the chance of having a real Independent in the Senate. They could not imagine *not* having their marionettes at their disposal.

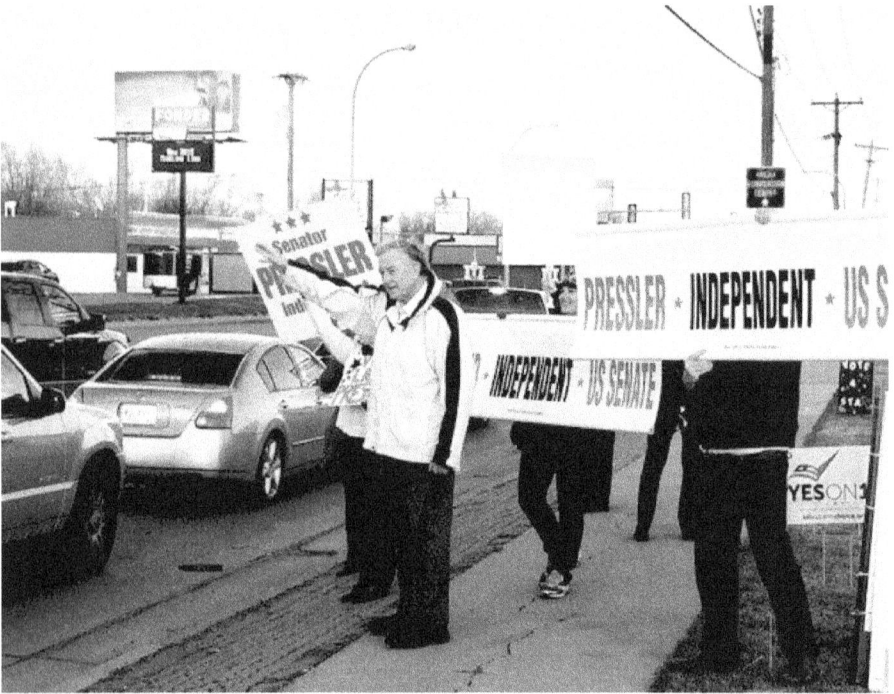

We campaigned at a major intersection right up until the polls closed. Photo - Larry Pressler.

Did I peak too early? Perhaps. We will never know. I took a calculated risk to spend my small media budget before Labor Day during the summer political advertising vacuum. In retrospect, it might have been a strategic mistake because my ascension in the polls alerted my enemies and triggered the blitzkrieg that rained down upon me. Had I spent my limited resources in the final four weeks of the campaign, I might not have suffered so much abuse at the hands of my opponents. But my positive message would have been lost in the political advertising clutter of the campaign season. So, as President Ulysses S. Grant observed, it is much easier to fight a battle strategically after it is over than to plan one in advance!

Shortly after the polls closed at 8:00 p.m., all the national media called the election and announced that the Republican, former Governor Mike Rounds, was the winner. Only slightly more than half the eligible voters turned out at the polls. I made a concession call to Mike shortly thereafter: "Hi Mike. It is Larry Pressler calling to congratulate you... We had an interesting race and you are going to do well down there in the Senate and if there is anything I can do to help you, tell me...you're my senator now...thank you and tell your family hello and your dad especially, okay?" (Senator Rounds' dad was a personal friend of mine).

The following day, a radio announcer opined, "Pressler won all the debates and got all the endorsements, but Rounds clearly got the votes." Unfortunately, most of the endorsements came very late. I think that was because newspapers wanted to keep getting the advertising revenues from both the Democrats and Republicans. The spigot might have been shut off if they endorsed an Independent candidate too early. I was barely buying any newspaper ads, so it must have been especially hard for them to endorse me.

At 9:00 p.m., I issued a statement:

> We may have lost this campaign at the polls today, but I feel that we have won by running to end the poisonous gridlock in Washington and incorporating South Dakota issues into the race. And I'm going to continue working on these issues with The Centrist Project and in my teaching in South Dakota universities.
>
> When I began this journey nearly two years ago, one of my co-chairmen, Don Frankenfeld of Rapid City, and I sat down and decided that we would have a good, issues- oriented campaign, on a low budget of individual contributors, but we'd offer

the people of the state a positive, issues-oriented campaign. We did that.

I want to thank the volunteer MVP of this campaign, my wife Harriet. She was with me every step of the way from helping drive to events, doing the campaign's accounting, answering phones, and thanking so many of the small contributors. She is a trooper.

What happened at the end of this campaign is exactly why we started this campaign. We were hit with a tsunami of negative ads from the Republican and Democratic parties and their affiliates. More money was spent in the last week against me than was raised in my entire campaign.

I thank all my supporters for their hard work, and look forward to continuing the crusade I started in this campaign. I am very grateful to all my contributors. Had this race just been decided by South Dakotans, we would have won. But we were hit with a deluge of out-of-state negative ads that distorted the outcome.

We received wonderful feedback in the immediate aftermath of my defeat. People continue to stop me at airports and on the street to tell me what a great campaign I ran. Although I would have liked to have seen a different outcome, I felt really good about the campaign we had run. I wasn't bitter; it isn't in my nature to be bitter. I have chosen to turn the other cheek in times like this. Running and losing took all the spiritual strength I had, but I think of myself as a modern-day Job. Perhaps it stems from my values and all the hard knocks in life I have overcome. It certainly gives me more empathy for others.

Losing a race for the U.S. Senate is very hard. I was bruised and smarting, but I had lost before, especially when my political nemesis, Democratic Senator Tim Johnson, narrowly defeated me in a sharply fought and very costly campaign in 1996—the most expensive campaign in South Dakota history at the time. I was running for a fourth term, and the loss was especially hard because I was chairman of the Senate Commerce Committee. But I moved forward then and I didn't look back. In fact, I even voted for and endorsed Senator Johnson in 2008!

In 2006, Senator Johnson had been hospitalized for a brain hemorrhage, which resulted in a permanent speech impediment. Harriet and I visited him in the hospital and later in his D.C. office. He later won reelection in 2008 and served as the chairman of the Senate Banking Committee. Although his voice was always halting, his mind was unfailingly clear. I just admired so much Johnson's courage to keep going despite his difficulty. Naturally, I felt a strong connection with his problem, understanding all too well the horrible frustration of having something to say and not being able to say it. Moreover, I wanted him to know he was still my fellow South Dakotan and fellow American. We look out for each other.

As a result, veteran South Dakota journalist Kevin Woster unexpectedly wrote a powerful column in the *Rapid City Journal*, "Pressler gives state a lesson in moving on," and it is one of the most remembered articles in South Dakota.

Woster wrote extensively about what he felt was my surprising endorsement of Senator Johnson, which had shaken the South Dakota political establishment at the time. He quoted me as saying: "I feel gloriously liberated from a lot of my old political grudges. I told Harriet just the other day that getting to know Tim, having a prayer with him and voting for him was the best thing I did this year. It's not that big a deal, but it sure makes me feel good." Woster apparently thought it was a big deal and concluded in his article that I gave our state "a lesson in moving on that more of us should follow."

It is my observation that a person's success is more judged by how he handles defeats and setbacks in life. Everybody has successes and setbacks—and we usually write about or hear about the successes. But dealing with the defeats, great or small, is more important. In the prayer *Our Father*, the sentence that says "Thy will be done" is my refuge. This prayer has taught me to trust in God and move on after a setback.

So I went to sleep the night of November 4 with an easy conscience, knowing I had given this campaign my best shot and knowing that I had maintained my integrity. I had no regrets. I also knew that I would indeed move on from this experience and that God would show me my next steps.

The question I asked myself when I woke up the morning after the election is: Did I make a difference?

CHAPTER 21

We Scared 'Em!

"We scared 'em!" That was the assessment of one national figure who observed the insidious attacks on me from all sides in late October. Both parties had a visceral response to my (almost) successful campaign effort. Their attack ads, mailings, emails, and robocalls worked. I lost the election. The Republicans dominated the election cycle all across the country that year—in part a reaction to the whipped-up frenzy and hatred toward President Obama, and in part due to the fact that 2014 was a midterm election with a very low turnout. In almost any other year, experts believe I would have won.

Not content with the brutal and irrational offensive on my campaign, the party establishment also wanted to prevent another campaign like mine from getting so close to the finish line. Shortly after my November defeat, the South Dakota Senate introduced and passed several amendments to Senate Bill 69 (SB 69). This bill prohibits any registered Republican or Democrat from signing a petition to get an Independent candidate on the ballot in my state. Under this amendment, only Independents would be allowed to sign petitions in support of Independent candidates. This amendment is a concerted effort to protect the major parties' influence over the political process in my state. In fact, many states are attempting similar measures to make it harder for Independents to get on the ballot. Ironically, on this issue, the two parties are working toward the same goal—to preserve their duopoly. Doesn't it sound like my campaign scared them?

My friend Jacqueline Salit, president of Independent Voting.org and the author of the book *Independents Rising*, characterized SB 69 this way: Larry's performance "was an early warning bell to the political establishment in South Dakota. The Republican Party [and the Democratic Party!] went to work to try to figure out what they were going to do in order to try to stuff the genie back in the bottle. Larry didn't win the election, but he demonstrated that an Independent leader, an Independent candidate with a reform philosophy and with a vision of putting American politics on a truly democratic rather than a partisan footing could, over time, defeat the parties...."

Jackie has built a large network of Independent leaders and activists in the country. She ran Michael Bloomberg's Independent campaign in New York City. She and I are kindred spirits on this issue and she gave me some solid advice throughout the campaign. Jackie is now trying to put together a repeal referendum on the ballot in 2016 to override the actions of the South Dakota legislature. Let's put this issue in front of the voters and let *them* decide—not the state parties.

"The whole point of the Independent movement and the whole point of being an Independent is to create something different, to create something that's non-hierarchical, that's genuinely and radically democratic," Jackie has said. "I think the tripwire that he set off through his candidacy last year put in motion this blowback from the parties... But anywhere you go in the country, the party in power will always be the one that gives you blowback.... But I thank him deeply for creating the situation that produced this blowback, which then caused this debate or this dialog to go on inside the Independent movement, which is fundamental and critical to everything that this movement is about. So I think the impact of this candidacy was gigantic."

Charles Wheelan, a professor at Dartmouth College and the

founder of The Centrist Project, issued a statement the day after the election:

> Change doesn't happen overnight but we made great inroads in 2014. Together, we woke America up to the possibility that there is a way to fix Washington. We endorsed and supported five centrist candidates for US Senate, including three running as Independents without the benefits of a big-party label... Lesson number one from our work for Independents Greg Orman of Kansas and Larry Pressler of South Dakota: Credible independent candidates can get traction in statewide races. We will see more of them. Voters are fed up with the two-party status quo and will embrace a candidate who vows to get things done and work against partisanship. Lesson number two: Come Election Day, the parties will fight back mercilessly. Like any duopoly with a stranglehold on power, the two parties are going to hang on tight, even as the proportion of Americans who support one party or the other steadily dwindles. Something has to change...

The Pew Research Center has cited statistics confirming that, as of June 2015, 45 percent of Americans identify themselves as Independents. With numbers that high, we need elected officials who look more like our electorate. But our two political parties dismiss us. They allege that we are not really independent at all. They are wrong. They just put all kinds of barriers in place to prevent Independent candidates from getting on the ballot, raising money, and focusing on the issues! For these political parties and their very large donors, it's really all about preserving their power and influence.

Which brings me to the topic of fundraising and the dominance of special interests. Most of the books you read about campaign finance reform, and the television talking heads pontificating about this issue, loudly propose a "silver bullet" solution to the money problem in Washington. According to them, it's easy. Just pass a constitutional amendment granting Congress the power to limit expenditures.

I agree, but it's not likely to happen and we should be honest with ourselves. A constitutional amendment of this nature would be almost impossible to pass because the exact same special-interest groups would oppose it and Americans are very sensitive about any measure that would affect the First Amendment. More significant, even if a constitutional amendment were to pass, Congress would still have to adopt the implementing legislation to set the spending limits. Members of Congress have shown no willingness to do that in the past and there is no indication that they would do so in the future.

Another alternative proposed is a major change in Supreme Court membership. I agree, but there is no guarantee that new Supreme Court members will do anything differently, even if a committed president could get these members confirmed in the Senate. And there is no guarantee that new Supreme Court justices will not change their minds once on the bench.

Yet another solution might be to adopt the California "top two primary," which passed in the state in 2010. Also called a "blanket primary," the law eliminated the political parties' separate primaries. All candidates for federal office run in one primary, at the same time, regardless of their political affiliation. The top two finishers advance to the general election. Some say it has resulted in more centrist- leaning nominees and has reduced the number of extremists who must pass the parties' purity tests to be nominated.

Others say it has made the primaries more expensive,

making money even more influential. In other words, the results have been mixed.

Another variation to this idea is holding "open primaries" at the state level, where citizens can choose to vote in any primary—regardless of their party affiliation. This process tends to favor more moderate candidates, so the state parties oppose it.

In another interesting proposal, several politicians around the country are trying to change *the source* of campaign funding. In other words, they want to see a migration from *large-dollar private funding* to *small-dollar public funding*. Maryland Democratic Representative John Sarbanes has introduced a bill that would match—up to 9 to 1—small, individual donations with tax credits. Others have proposed tax rebates in exchange for accepting public funding. Up to thirteen states have "clean election" laws on the books, offering subsidies to candidates who pledge to limit their spending and private funding. Supporters of these proposals allege that this would substantially increase the number of funders in campaigns and reduce the concentration and influence of large funders. However, when offered the opportunity, the American public has demonstrated its unwillingness to donate even one dollar to public financing on their tax returns. Even though I would support this idea with my pocketbook, most Americans wouldn't.

Finally, some have entertained the idea of a national electoral commission as a possible solution. This could be in the form of a bipartisan commission, set up like a military base closure commission, that is responsible for settling election disputes and putting limits on spending. But since this would still be a commission that would probably be appointed by a partisan president, and the commission's recommendations would have to be voted on by Congress, I don't see this as a workable solution either.

While these are all promising ideas, they really just nibble at the edges of the larger problem, and it is irresponsible to tout these proposals as solutions. They are not innovative solutions and they are not likely to happen. What will really change Washington?

CHAPTER 22

My Solutions

T he following four solutions would represent a disruptive innovation in American politics. I believe we should make it our mission to make these changes.

First, we must elect three to five Independent U.S. Senators, which would be a fundamental innovative change in American politics. The Senate is a fulcrum. It is the most powerful central force in our nation today. Our various departments and agencies are also paralyzed due to the poisonous partisanship between Democrats and Republicans. That paralysis throughout the U.S. government would be broken if we had a third force in the U.S. Senate. We must get a small critical mass of Independents elected there—free of special interests. I am a member of The Centrist Project's Founding Circle and support their effort to elect three to five Independent senators in the 2016 and 2018 election cycles. Our model is the current Maine Independent Senator Angus King. It was and remains my conviction that this is a true solution to the deadlock in American politics. But a recalibration of the Senate's power balance is only one piece of the solution.

Second, we must institute a universal service requirement in America to fight the malaise that is affecting our nation. Restore a universal service concept for military and public service with a new twist—a staggered lottery. Make it as fair as humanly possible by making it truly universal—for men and women—and make the service concept mandatory.

As I campaigned around my state in 2014, in both my speeches and personal encounters, I would use every opportunity I had to recommend a new national public service program in this country—not just military service, but national public service. Why? So that every young American will have a vested interest in our country. I feel that this could enable my generation to heal the lingering wounds from the flawed Vietnam-era draft that tore us apart. In my opinion, this type of universal service would bring us together.

My dad served a year in the Civilian Conservation Corps (CCC) in the 1930s. He planted trees in western South Dakota and in Wyoming. He took great pride in the fact that he had helped President Franklin D. Roosevelt fight the Great Depression in his small way. Public service was in my DNA.

When I had an opportunity to avoid the draft with a legal student deferment, I'm proud of the fact that I chose to volunteer for Vietnam. My dad advised me to do so, so I felt then and I feel now that it was my civic duty. At the time I faced the draft, everyone was expected to serve his country for a few years. It was the obligation that came with citizenship in this country. Now, we have a career-oriented, professional fighting-force class comprising less than 1 percent of our nation's citizens. Now, the only obligations of citizenship are jury duty and paying taxes—yet most people seem to find a way to get out of jury duty and many avoid paying taxes.

Some say that a new type of draft for public service would cause more problems than it would solve and would create a massive jobs program that would be unwieldy to manage. That is not true, and I speak with some recent authority, having just completed service on President Obama's and Congress's Military Compensation and Modernization Commission. I can assure you that such a universal service program would save a great deal of money and perform many essential tasks in our society.

The cornerstone of a successful program to instill a sense of civic obligations in today's youth is a fair and practical universal service requirement—one with no exceptions, no exemptions, no deferments. The program could be managed by a "no-escape," staggered lottery system and would serve several purposes: it would enlist young people for military conscription or other community services domestically and abroad to serve our national needs and obligations.

Aside from military service, young civilians could perform a host of other service projects. They could work with our growing senior population; they could provide law enforcement, firefighting, or emergency medical support; they could repair our crumbling bridges and pave our roads or replant forests; they could help overworked teachers; they could support medical professionals in hospitals and nursing homes; or they could assist city and county clean-up crews.

Bipartisan support for programs like these already exists; many legislators have introduced similar community service initiatives. Republican Senator John McCain and Democratic Senator Michael Bennet have recently introduced legislation that would establish a twenty-first century CCC. Democratic Senator Edward Kennedy introduced the Serve America Act in 2009, which called for an increase in national service programs. President George W. Bush introduced the USA Freedom Corps after 9/11. And, in place for decades are the Peace Corps, Teach for America, FEMA Corps, AmeriCorps, and many others.

Beyond the actual tasks performed, and the benefits of those tasks, the most important consequence of such a universal service requirement would be substantial changes in our public policy and national mindset. Right from the start, I predict, the United States would get involved in fewer optional wars. If substantial numbers of parents stood the chance of having their children drafted and sent into combat, I suspect our national leaders would become far more cautious about "discretionary" adventures overseas and unnecessary spending here at home. Further, if every young person performed some public service, we could restore the respectability of—even the aspiration toward— public service. In my opinion, it would also result in higher voter turnout and voter engagement in the electoral process. Knowing their sons' and daughters' futures were at stake, the mothers of America would never miss a vote.

Third, we must immediately pass a statute that prohibits lobbyists from making campaign contributions. This includes broadening the definition of lobbying to include anyone who is trying to influence public policy. Without a change to this legal corruption, all the other changes will be irrelevant. We must get lobbyists out of the fundraising business. My friend Tom Patton, a prominent Washington, D.C., lawyer, recommends that those who register as lobbyists would not be able to raise money for political candidates. This proposal could separate lobbyists from fundraising and could help to break the power of the lobbyist- driven money machine in Washington. Lobbyists would still lobby on the merits of legislation, but they would not be able to use money to influence legislators. The advantage to this proposal is that Congress could pass it as a statute, as Congress has the authority to define categories of citizens through the internal revenue code. This statutory change should also include changing our nation's bribery statutes to eliminate the massive influence peddling that occurs during the election season. It would not require a constitutional amendment. The disadvantage is that lobbyists would oppose it—but we must overcome that. To simplify this concept, it would mean that lobbyists and donors have a choice: they can be one or the other, but not both.

There is a constitutional precedent at the state level, in Wisconsin. Registered lobbyists in the Wisconsin state legislature cannot make political contributions to anybody between election day and the end of the subsequent legislative session—a period of about ten months.

Fourth, above and beyond step 2, we must trigger a general reawakening, reeducation, and revival of citizens' civic duties. This "revival" must include individual and collective civic service—something this Millennial generation currently has no obligation to do. Recently, I asked a college audience of about forty students how many had voted in the recent midterm elections. Six hands went up, which was about what I anticipated. What I did not expect was the discussion that followed. The students stated that not voting was a matter of pride, as they did not want to validate a corrupt, meaningless process in which their vote meant little. That same attitude has been expressed to me by many voters. This is something new in American politics—pride and idealism in not voting. Hearing it broke my heart.

Very frankly, I was disappointed by the voters in my state for not turning out. Citizens continue to complain about corruption in politics, partisan bickering, and a lack of qualified candidates to win. But very few citizens will do anything to educate themselves about the candidates and the issues—much less take the time to vote. In general, the public is lazy and apathetic about politics.

Therefore, a more fundamental change of attitude is crucial. But we will have to take some specific steps to lay a foundation for such a revival. What can we voluntarily do to encourage more participation in the electoral process and really listening to candidates—not just for national office, but for county and state offices, too? How can we inspire higher quality candidates to run for office? What can we do to instill more pride in serving the public good?

Unfortunately, budget cuts have sabotaged basic civics courses; civics is just not taught anymore. We could adopt the approaches to civics education espoused by former Justice Sandra

Day O'Connor and Bill Gates. Justice O'Connor's program is called iCivics and provides school curriculum to engage students in creative ways to learn about our federal, state, and local governments. It also suggests a requirement for states to teach more civics. Civics would also be taught in vocational schools and a number of other contexts. Bill Gates tackles this issue on his New Learning website, and also funds organizations that teach civics.

Our citizens must wake up and really work toward a new era. We have had such periods of renewal in American history before—for example, the "Era of Good Feelings." This "era" took place shortly after the end of the War of 1812, when the country was swept by the mood of victory. This was a period during the nineteenth century when bitter partisan disputes were replaced with a trend toward unity and national purpose.

It can happen within one generation. Note how people feel about veterans and the military today versus the 1970s. When I served in Vietnam, I was told not to wear my uniform in public in the United States because some people would actually spit on it. The public took out their anger about America's foreign policy on any soldier. Today, there is an innate understanding of the difference between the war and the warrior. The public now understands that they can disagree with the war, but still love the warrior. That perceptual shift is 180 degrees from when I served.

Most important, *we should all have a role to play* to keep our republic strong and our elected representatives honest. Perhaps this idea could contribute to a "disruptive innovation" in politics, one my friend Clayton Christensen of the Harvard Business School's innovation theory might envision. More than in any other part of our society, we need innovation and independent thinking in our political system—our mission is to save America.

CHAPTER 23

Winning by Losing

D
id my Independent candidacy do any good? Was my campaign worth it? Did this really help my beloved state of South Dakota and our nation? Or was it just an exercise in self-centeredness—the efforts of an old man trying to grasp at restoring past glory? If I had it to do over again, would I run? Was it worth nearly two years of my life and about $450,000 dollars out of our retirement account?

A resounding "YES" came from South Dakotans and from people around the nation! Ironically, no previous campaign that I had won received more praise, compliments, editorials, and good feelings than my 2014 Independent campaign. Across the country, people universally noted the campaign, followed it in a level of detail that surprised me, and told me I had done a noble thing. One former U.S. senator told me he was secretly envious of me for getting on the campaign trail again and running such a good campaign. *I won by losing!*

Part of the reason I ran in 2014 was to get off my duff and take some action. Clayton Christensen, who baptized me as a Mormon, gave a speech to the Harvard Business School graduating class in 2010. He titled it: "How to Measure Your Life." It had a profound impact on me. Clayton adheres to his religion's ideal of living by a strong work ethic. He advised these ambitious graduate students to work with a higher purpose in mind. He talked about how work should be done in the service of others—

even in a business setting. He talked of measuring the value of life by broader things than just money earned. He talked of serving others. His thinking was one of my inspirations for running again—after so many years on the political sidelines.

I strongly believe that we all have to be politically active. That might involve running for office, it might involve volunteering for a political campaign, or it might involve attending a political meeting to truly understand the issues affecting everyday Americans—not just relying on thirty- second campaign ads. My pet peeve is the uneducated and apathetic voter: someone who determines how he will vote by sitting in an armchair with a beer in one hand and a TV remote in the other—listening uncritically to negative ads.

I regard a vote as a sacred right, just as I regard public service as a sacred obligation. Public service to me means service to God and mankind. I believe that public service is among the highest callings, and I think politics is part of that. Most people who run for office lose, but their campaigns can have a positive effect on issues. I'm confident mine did.

Despite defeat at the polls, we succeeded in my 2014 campaign because we set a new standard for decency and clean campaigning. We succeeded because I followed my calling to run and did absolutely everything I could to win—I was satisfied that I had followed my innermost spiritual drives. We succeeded because we helped bring South Dakota politics back to a more moderate stance: with two Republican senators now in office, neither has called for the repeal of Obamacare, and the inflammatory rhetoric to impeach Obama has gone away.

A year after the election, I visited The Centrist Project's national meeting in Chicago and was greeted as something of a celebrity. We have apparently set a new, higher standard for campaigns, and The Centrist Project is using my campaign as its model. Based on some of my recent campus visits, we have now ignited a nationwide interest in "running as an Independent."

Maybe I was ahead of my time. Maybe I envisioned something that is not yet apparent to our country. But I know I was a catalyst for change and I'm confident our country will solve its problems. And, by losing in 1996 and 2014, I won so many other things. So many opportunities for teaching and travel, so many friendships, so many experiences outside of elected office were afforded me when I lost. So, I never complain, as God always seems to bring me new challenges.

Abraham Lincoln lost his Senate race to Stephen Douglas, but the Lincoln-Douglas debates set a new national standard for Senate races. I would not dream of placing myself anywhere near the stature of Abraham Lincoln or Stephen Douglas, but I think in a small way my campaign as an Independent in 2014 had an impact far beyond winning or losing. I was able to speak out freely on issues without fear or party constraint. It was liberating.

I'm reminded that the four political figures etched on Mt. Rushmore in South Dakota were all Independents at some point in their careers. They took political risks and unpopular positions to benefit our great nation—not to advance their reputation or to line their pocketbooks. They were committed public servants and knew how to cross vast party chasms and create progress. We as a nation should still be able to produce politicians like that. I know we still can.

As I now look back on my 2014 campaign, I recognize it as one of the happiest times of my life. My friend and campaign chairman Don Frankenfeld was right: the journey was more important than the destination. I know my campaign has inspired other Independents to try to get elected. I know I demonstrated how an honest, issues- oriented campaign can resonate with voters. I know that a low-budget campaign can be successful. I know I took the high road when the Republican and Democratic parties didn't. I know I followed my heart, and it set me free.

An Independent Mission

Free at last, free at last!
Great God Almighty,
Free at last!

--Isaiah 25

COWBOY'S PRAYER

In times of stress, I sometimes like to envision that I am a cowboy on a horse out herding cattle in the moonlight. I imagine myself looking up into the night sky, where I have a direct conversation with God. Many cowboys didn't go to church because they were out on the prairies looking after animals, but real cowboys have a reputation for a lot of "Job"-like conversations with God. Here is one example:

Cowboy's Prayer

Our Heavenly Father, we pause at this time,
Mindful of the many blessings you have bestowed upon us.
We ask, Lord, that you will be with us in the arena of life.
We as cowboys do not ask for special favors.
We don't ask to draw around the chute fighting horse, the
     steer that won't lay, or to never break the barrier.
We don't even ask for all daylight runs.
We do ask, Lord, that you will help us live our lives here on
earth as cowboys, in such a manner, that when we make
     that last inevitable ride, to the country up there, where
     the grass grows lush, green, and stirrup high, and the
     water runs cool, clear, and deep, that you'll take us by
     the hand and say—
"Welcome to Heaven cowboy, your entry fees are paid."

Based on Clem McSpadden's "Cowboy's Prayer"

AUTHOR'S BIOGRAPHY

F ormer Senator Larry Pressler was born and raised on a farm in South Dakota. He became a 4-H standout as a teenager when he delivered the organization's national report to President Kennedy in the Oval Office, and was the first in his family to attend college. From the University of South Dakota, Pressler went on to Oxford on a Rhodes Scholarship, which he interrupted to enlist in the U.S. Army and serve two combat tours in Vietnam. He earned graduate degrees from Oxford, Harvard's Kennedy School of Government and Harvard Law School, and became a Foreign Service Officer. Running for Congress on a shoestring, he was elected twice to the House of Representatives, then later ran on his record as a champion of veterans' rights to win a seat in the U.S. Senate, where he represented South Dakota for three terms.

As a freshman senator, Pressler launched a short-lived presidential campaign and, while struggling for campaign contributions, was offered a $50,000 cash bribe by undercover FBI agents in a sting operation. Refusing the bribe made him the hero of the "ABSCAM" scandal, which sent one senator and five congressmen to jail for corruption. Among his signature achievements, he authored the "Pressler Amendment," which briefly halted the spread of nuclear weapons during the Reagan/Bush years, and he was the principal author of the epochal Telecommunications Act of 1996 which enabled the start of the Internet. His previously published books are *U.S. Senators from the Prairie* (University of South Dakota, 1982) and *Star*

Wars: The Strategic Defense Initiative Debates in Congress (introduction by James R. Schlesinger, Praeger, 1986).

Active on the lecture circuit, Pressler has held two visiting professorships as a Fulbright scholar, and often teaches as an adjunct professor. After being registered as both a Democrat and a Republican at different points in his life, he abandoned both parties and became a registered Independent in 2014.

Forty years after his first shoestring campaign, he ran another one—determined to break the poisonous deadlock in Congress.

A husband, father, and grandfather, he divides his time between Washington, D.C., and South Dakota.

Senator Larry Pressler

IN CLOSING

One result of this book has been an enormous number of invitations for me to speak to business/labor/civic groups—nationally and internationally—on inspiring citizens to actively participate in the governing of their countries. In fact, today I leave on a trip to India to speak in five cities. In March, I shall lecture and interact with students for a full week at Brigham Young University in Provo, Utah and in autumn of this year at my alma mater, Harvard Law School. Throughout the year I will also speak to five major business/civic groups.

I thank God that I have the energy, the ability, the inspiration, and the enthusiasm to speak about presidential politics, U.S. Senate races, ethics in business, and the struggle to improve our society. If you have any comments on this book or would like to be in touch with me to speak to your organization, my contact information is below. I would love to hear from you and to speak to your group, too!

Larry Pressler
February 10, 2016

CONTACT INFORMATION:

SENATOR LARRY PRESSLER (RET.)
THE PLAZA, SUITE 504
800 25TH STREET, NW
WASHINGTON, DC 20037-2208
LPRESSLER@LARRYPRESSLER.COM
WWW.LARRYPRESSLER.COM

www.ingramcontent.com/pod-product-compliance
Lightning Source LLC
Chambersburg PA
CBHW032000040426
42448CB00006B/433